Nuts,

Bolts,

& Jolts

Fundamental Business and Life Lessons You Must Know

RICHARD A. MORAN

ROOFTOP
publishing

Rooftop Publishing™
1663 Liberty Drive, Suite 200
Bloomington, IN 47403
Phone: 1-800-839-8640

©2006   Richard A. Moran. All rights reserved

No part of this book may be reproduced, stored in a retrieval system, or transmitted by any means without the written permission of the author.

First published by Rooftop Publishing™ 09/26/2006

ISBN: 1-60008-015-4 (sc)

Printed in the United States of America
Bloomington, Indiana

This book is printed on acid-free paper.

There is an infinite well of stories and aphorisms that will continue to float to the surface as business life changes and the gadgets that we all use change. (My earlier books talked about pagers like they would last forever.) Thanks to all those who send in suggestions and thanks to all those friends who observe crazy behavior and insights and say, "There's one for Moran's books." Most of all, I am grateful for the changes in the workplace, which make for a constant set of situations where people might struggle over the right thing to do. I am happy to create a path of light that may illuminate what's important and how one should act.

Special thanks to Brett Azuma for insightful contributions and to my editor, Lesley Bolton, and Kevin King at Rooftop Publishing.

Thanks to all those out there who are slugging it out every day trying to put in a good day's work for a fair wage.

To the family,

Carol, Brady, Scott, Megan, and John,

all of whom have written bullets down for me
so I wouldn't forget them.

CONTENTS

INTRODUCTION

I have often told the story that I wrote most of my first book, *Never Confuse a Memo with Reality*, one night while on an airplane from New York to San Francisco. It went on to become a bestseller. It was a very long and productive flight.

When I began that trip, I hadn't intended to write a book. I was in New York City for only a day. During that one fateful day, several events pushed me into becoming a business author and creating a genre of "business books of bullets." First, during an interview over breakfast for a very senior position, the job candidate told me I looked like a golden retriever. I barked in response. Later that morning, at a meeting with financial analysts, my client droned through a presentation and repeatedly said, "I know you can't read this, but…" Indeed, no one could see, so they stopped paying attention and got on their cell phones and BlackBerries. Even later, a different client gave a presentation to his own marketing group while wearing a shirt that didn't fit. Without the benefit of a T-shirt, his hairy belly was sticking out through the buttons of the shirt. His gross hairy belly was all anyone saw or paid attention to.

After a day like that, I needed something to stop me from talking to myself or drinking heavily on the return flight. I needed a cathartic event to make me feel better. So on that airplane ride from East to West Coast, I poured my heart into the laptop. It became a list of rules "too simple not to know." I wondered, "Is it just me, or do people just not know that there are simple rules to follow to be successful in business and in their careers and lives?" Turns out, people are looking for those rules.

While chatting with a fellow business traveler on a flight right after that first book was published, he told me that my book had changed his life. I was appreciative but suggested he should consider reading something else like *The Da Vinci Code* or *Harry Potter*. My books are not intended to change lives. They are intended to shed some light on what we are all dealing with in the workplace and improve our lot there. Navigating through the worlds of work, family, and all the white space surrounding those two big categories is hard and stressful and demanding and time consuming. If truth and humor in my books will improve our chances to enjoy work, develop a career, and maintain a quality life, then my intentions with the books will be fulfilled.

My books are born of my own observations. The observations are formed through a very simple methodology: I watch people and listen to what they say at work. Most tell me what people at work already know. I spend time with people at work, while they are working. The locations can range from the tarmac at the airport in Pittsburgh, to the bank corporate headquarters in Los Angeles, to the steel mill in Chicago, the insurance company in Connecticut, and the high-tech company in San Jose.

Studs Terkel is the original one who captured a true sense of the work world, albeit not an inspiration for applying for jobs. His book, *Working*, is a masterpiece; however, it paints a pretty grim picture and provides little in the way of advice. It's hard to get up in the morning when Studs starts describing work. In the second sentence of *Working* he describes work as "about ulcers as well as accidents, about shouting matches as well as fistfights, about nervous breakdowns as well as kicking the dog around." I was okay until the dog. Why worry about performance reviews when your dog is getting all hell kicked out of him?

Scott Adams, through his *Dilbert* strip, is the new Studs Terkel, except he's funny. *Dilbert* has done more to tell the truth about work than all the latest business books combined. Although hilarious, *Dilbert* only shows what is, not how to improve it. There is no prescription from *Dilbert*.

The message I want to convey to my readers is that work isn't so bad. In fact, we all feel most fulfilled when we are productive at work. If it wasn't so, why do Bill Gates and other billionaires work? There are lots of things, some big, some small, that we can all do to improve our lives at work. That is what this book is all about.

The messages aren't complicated. Most people I know don't have the time or the inclination for sophisticated modeling to improve their lives. Hope, advice, and readability—people are looking for all three.

Most business books, I believe, are really five "bullets" of messages that get stretched into a book. The more powerful the bullets, the more successful the book. This is an entire book of bullets—prescriptions for you. The prescriptions may come in handy just in time and may bring a chuckle in your next meeting. Here we have a batch of new material and a categorized compilation of my other books—all boiled down.

The stories and bullets are put forth with the hope of making you more successful and to help you learn from others' mistakes. We all have biases about work. Two that I do not have are:

1. People are lazy and unwilling to change

2. All bosses are assholes with MBAs

Rather, my perspective is that almost all people are trying to do a good job and improve their organization and their own lot in life amid the struggles of work/life balance, financial pressures, and more esoteric questions like, Does what I do make a difference to anyone?

Solving complex problems with simple bullets or aphorisms is not realistic, nor is it my intent. Rather, I want to interpret what people are saying to get to the real heart of the issue *and* the solution. For example, when I hear people say, "The biggest problem this company has is communication," I doubt they want more meetings with management. What they are really saying is, "With all these changes, I'm not sure I even know what my job is anymore. All I do is drain E-mail and voice mail. Will someone please tell me what is happening?"

Or, when a CEO who is trying to manage a crazed organization says, "I'm not sure if I have the right people," what is really meant is, "We may have the right number of people here; I'm just not sure they are doing the right things."

The insights here are derived from countless meetings, interviews, focus groups, team training sessions, staff retreats, and from just being "on the floor." Nothing is made up; I am only synthesizing and repeating what others have told me.

So as you are settling in for a good read, relax and know that even in the introduction, there are some helpful bullets:

- Never answer your cell phone while in the bathroom.
- Tell the truth about what is really happening in the organization so that people can work on the right problems.

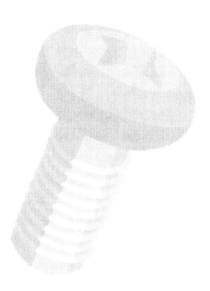

Refrigerator Rules - All That Counts

We've all learned to live within the rules, both formal and informal. At best, the rules make for an efficient well-oiled machine. At worst, they are constant reminders of why we would like to be somewhere, anywhere, else.

At a time when lots of people are virtual and there is so much turmoil in the workplace, it is more and more difficult to know what the new rules are. You won't find everything you need to know in the dreaded policies and procedures manual. Much of those manuals are geared to keep you and the organization out of jail or the court system. It goes without saying that you must pay attention to them. Showing up and complying with the rules of the federal and state government is always a good first step toward a good performance review. But there is another whole super-set of rules—some are standard, and some are unique to each organization. How you follow them or not creates your persona at work.

Once, I had a new boss who met with a colleague and me to introduce himself and his beliefs. He discussed integrity and work habits and so on, but the only part of the discussion I will ever remember is his story of his new office initiation. The new boss believed that since he worked long hours and spent so much time in the office without his wife she needed to be in the office for him spiritually—her essence needed to be there for him. So, he said, he would steal her in on a weekend and make love to her on his desk.

He was no prize to look at, and the image was frightening. During his tenure in the job, which wasn't long, I was never able to sit across his desk from him and hear a word he said. This behavior was probably not singled out in the Employee Manual, but how he interpreted rules of judgment set his persona.

Knowing the informal rules and following them is, in many ways, similar to manners. Not knowing manners or not paying attention to them will, in most cases, have you breaking the informal rules left and right. William Wickham, the founder of England's Winchester school, said, "Manners maketh the man." Man or woman, the phrase still holds, and how you interpret manners and rules makes both you and the community at work better.

A few examples of things not to do: Taking the newspaper to the bathroom with you and hanging out in there for a long time; looking at inappropriate Web sites (you know which ones they are); long personal calls; not being responsive; slouching in the lobby while waiting for an appointment; talking on your cell phone when you're with someone else; taking supplies; anything that *Dilbert* says is wrong…

The list of what not to do is long, but the real point to remember is that people notice. If you are a boar, people do notice and think less of you for it. People will form perceptions about your work based on your ability to create good rules and live up to them.

The one and only rule that is universally enforced and the one that keeps people's attention is about the food in the refrigerator. In fact, I have often said it is the only corporate initiative that is always implemented well. When you see the sign that says, "This refrigerator will be emptied every Friday," you pay attention because you don't want to lose that old coleslaw.

⚒ Easy projects, easy sales, or hot new business opportunities are like children's soccer; everyone clusters around the ball.

⚒ Squatter's rights don't count when it comes to reserved conference rooms.

⚒ Use no more than two of the following words in the same sentence: value, delivery, quality, strategic, global, or paradigm.

- One size fits all is never true, especially with hats.

- Don't speak on a cell phone on the sidelines of your child's game unless the cell phone is what allows you to be there.

- Being efficient could mean that you end your day with zero unopened E-mails or unanswered voice mails. Being effective means you measured your day in what you accomplished, not in E-mails and voice mails.

- The best thing about making lists of things to do is the ability to cross things off.

- If you accomplish something significant that is not on your list, write it down so you can cross it off.

- Eating in your car is the most effective way to gain weight. Doughnuts, burgers, and french fries are the meals of choice.

- "Okay" is not a punctuation mark. It should not be substituted for a comma, a question mark, or the question "Are you with me?"

- Surfing between job-hunting Web sites and porno Web sites will leave you confused.

- Buzzwords are like Top 40 songs. At first they bring a smile or capture a thought, but you are soon sick of them. Think value-added paradigms.

- Quick hits and low-hanging fruit are never as quick or as low as everyone believes.

- Beware those who ask for feedback. They are really asking for compliments.

- Employees are best at implementing strategies, not setting them.

- When you oversleep, spend an extra minute in bed to develop a recovery plan.

- On a bad-weather day when there is no work, either play in the snow and have fun with the kids or try to work from home as best you can. Don't get uptight about things you can't control, such as the weather.

- When everyone in the company walks around carrying a calculator, it means employees believe an early retirement plan is about to be announced.

- Don't gossip. Don't do things that make you a party to gossip or the subject of gossip.

- Avoid "Long-Term Parking" at all costs.

- It's better to look bad than to smell bad.
- The higher the level of a manager referring a job candidate, the worse the candidate.
- Don't wear turquoise pinkie rings.
- Ignore any new fashion trend with its roots in the 1960s or 1970s.
- Use the phrase "value-added" no more than once a week. Never use paradigms.
- If you alphabetize your CDs, remember that most of the world doesn't work that way.
- No matter how late you work, always arrive at work on time.
- The sun will always shine on your computer screen when you don't want it to.
- A split-second is the time between when you stub your toe and when it hurts. That's how long it takes to make a decision.
- Always keep the ball in their court.
- Use "ASAP" only when it's urgent.

✳   The number of calls you receive is directly proportional to the number of calls you make.

✳   Go to any meeting where food is served. If something productive also gets done in the meeting, it's a bonus.

✳   If someone who works for you resigns, the meeting does not need to take more than five minutes.

✳   Those who refuse to play office politics can be at the mercy of those who do. At least understand the game and the rules.

✳   Never wordsmith in a meeting. You probably have better things to do.

✳   The fear of being dull is not a bad fear.

✳   Early retirement opportunities should always be explored. Talk to an actuary if you don't understand it.

✳   Remember what it was like to show up in the classroom on test day to see a substitute teacher and learn the test was postponed? That should occasionally be duplicated at work.

✳   Lean and mean does not equate with productive and satisfied.

- Work long hours, maintain a meaningful relationship, and raise great kids is a recipe that has never worked, and its prospects for working are dimmer all the time.

- "Civil service mentality" is never used to describe a highly effective and efficient work group.

- Monday-morning staff meetings are dangerous and not as effective as ones later in the week.

- If you schedule a Monday breakfast meeting, make sure you get home phone numbers.

- If your checkbook never balances, change banks.

- It's a cliché to say, "In our rapidly changing society (economy, world, technology...)"; everyone knows it.

- Not being able to take your vacation when you want to or need to is bad for mental health and performance reviews.

- Never doodle something X-rated or about other people in the room. They are likely to see it.

- Never forgetting who your friends are is a good thing to be known for.

- Wearing Old Spice will remind everyone around you of their dads.

✗ Two words to be avoided in any conversation at work are *panties* and *silly*.

✗ When you are put on hold, put it on the speaker and get other things done. Don't sit there and stew.

✗ The "Hokey Pokey" is what it's all about.

✗ The support staff is still the backbone of almost all organizations.

✗ Presentations don't have to be fancy to be effective. It's not the technology; it's the message.

✗ Leaving notes instructing others to clean up after themselves won't clean up the mess. Use bigger threats or hire a custodian.

✗ Don't carry your spill-proof coffee cup around all day.

✗ People can tell by watching you on the phone, without hearing you, whether you're talking to a customer or your mom.

✗ Never assume that the amount you receive back will equal what you submit on your expense account.

✗ Overnight packages sent Saturday delivery are usually read on Monday morning.

✘ "Let's not tell them and maybe they'll never find out" always backfires at work. It's not different from when you were a kid.

✘ Stamina is an underrated attribute for business success.

✘ Special approvals make for special delays.

✘ Expect faxes and printouts to be missing if they are not picked up within fifteen minutes.

✘ Lack of credibility will hurt you more than lack of quality.

✘ When someone says, "Something good is about to happen to you," get ready to buy something.

✘ When employees start complaining about the company gym, they're probably spoiled.

✘ Pay fluctuations based on geography are never seen as fair.

✘ Rock bottom is always deeper than you think.

✘ When all else has failed, return to the basics.

✘ Pay your parking tickets, even if you get them in rental cars in far-away-from-home cities. They will catch up to you.

- Learn how not to lose things, to avoid insanity. Learn especially how not to lose checkbooks and credit cards.

- When you hear anything close to "We're not going to get any smarter about this," just make the decision.

- If you have to ask if there's a conflict of interest, there probably is.

- Cash bonus checks as soon as you receive them.

- When the note on the refrigerator says it will be emptied this Friday, get your salad dressing. Cleaning the refrigerator is the one corporate initiative that's always fully implemented.

Cubicle Life

When it comes to thriving in the workplace, most of the rules that applied when you were a sophomore in that co-ed dorm are still good. In a nutshell: Give people space, don't steal, clean up after yourself, and in general don't be a jerk are all you have to know. Oh, one more thing, do the work assigned to you better than expected. If only everyone would pay attention to those simple rules.

A lot of the world looks at the workplace as "my time spent in a cubicle." A cubicle is not a cell. It is an invention that inexpensively maximizes efficiency and allows your neighbor to overhear your fights with your mother on the telephone. Like it or not, the cubicle and the computer screen define much of the workplace today.

A friend recently received a promotion that would allow her to have her very own cubicle, no longer having to share too much of the lives and eating habits of her two former cube mates. She was determined to make her new home professional but have her own mark on it. As she started to move in, she wanted to put a few important items in the drawer that would be directly between her lap and her laptop, that prime real estate reserved for the special numbers and photos. When she opened the "special" drawer, she spied in small compartments at the front of the drawer a sight that had her ready to barf and quit her job. There were thousands, maybe millions, of fingernail clippings there in those little desk drawer compartments. It made her long for her old cube mates.

For many, it's difficult to tell where the workplace is located today. Being virtual might mean you have no idea where your workplace is even located. In that case, pretend you are working somewhere with someone in an ideal situation. Otherwise, that virtual workplace can get pretty lonesome.

The real world of the workplace is full of people who want to do well, make a living, develop relationships with their coworkers, and enjoy showing up in the morning. Knowing the rules and constraints will make the workplace much more enjoyable to you and those around you. In so many ways, the relationships developed in the workplace can be as rewarding as those developed at any other time in your life.

- If you're going to project a computer onto a large screen, make sure one of your icons is not labeled "porn."
- Expect that anything you leave in a virtual office is fair game to be picked through or stolen. Don't decorate a virtual office.
- If you come across a "personal" drawer in a virtual office (of the once-full-time inhabitant), leave it alone.
- If you wear six-inch heels, don't complain about them.
- "Gotta minute?" is a signal for an interruption coming.
- "Gimme a minute" is a signal that you can wait.
- Doors on offices that are REQUIRED to be open defeat the purpose of doors.
- Quick hits and low-hanging fruit are long gone. They were never as easy to achieve as they seemed anyway.
- At company birthday parties, remember that the colored napkins will always transfer colors onto your face and clothes.
- Innovation *can* happen without additional headcount. Just let it.

✗   Bumper stickers not to post in your cubicle:
    ⊘ Jesus is coming; everyone look busy.
    ⊘ Reality is a crutch for people who can't
       handle drugs.
    ⊘ My kid had sex with your honor student.
    ⊘ If you're not outraged, you're not paying attention.

✗   If your job is like playing "Bop the Mole," remember
     that even though they all pop up, not all moles are
     the same size. Just keep the hammer ready for the
     most important and lucrative moles.

✗   Fix your computer setup so you don't have to crawl
     around under your desk to plug it in. Doubly
     important if you have to get dressed up for work.

✗   Going virtual and hoteling make it easier to quit because
     you don't have to worry about cleaning out your office.

✗   When the family photos and children's art starts to
     disappear, that person is about to quit or knows he or
     she is about to get fired.

✗   You can be sure that consultants are on-site if four
     people wearing expensive sunglasses, all about
     thirty years old, show up in an American four-door
     sedan carrying briefcases. The alternative is that the
     president of the United States will soon be there.

- Even though you are getting spammed with reports of Viagra and body part enlargement, leave those stories at home.

- There are two kinds of people at work:
  - Those who take notes at every meeting and those who never do.
  - Those who read *PARADE* magazine and those who don't.
  - Those who answer the phone and those who put it on voice mail even if they are sitting next to the phone.
  - Those who want to answer the phone and those who do.
  - Those who click and point on small screens and those who use spiral-bound notebooks.

- In the virtual world, never underestimate how important it is that people talk to each other. Not because they have to but because they want to and need to.

- Remove the ink stamp on the back of your hand that you got at the bar last night before you show up for work.

- Jabbing the elevator button incessantly will not make it appear faster. Go to the bathroom before you get on the elevator.

- Referring to latency periods is best left in the domain of art or sexual development, not work.

- The amount of input requested should be inversely proportional to the amount of time remaining to complete the task.

- Treat "temps" (temporary employees) like the guy your sister is dating. Treat him nicely because he may become your brother-in-law. If he is suddenly gone, don't say, "I never liked him anyway," because he may be back tomorrow.

- Even in a virtual office, show up. Just know what showing up means. It could mean conference calls, logging on to E-mail, discharging voice mail, or chitchatting with your assistant.

- Learn how to work at home without treating it like it's a day off.

- If you work at home a lot, don't talk about *Oprah* or *General Hospital* when you do show up.

- Sometimes it is easier and cheaper to try something and see what happens than to study and analyze it.

- Going virtual killed snow days. If you can work at home when it is sunny, you can work at home when it is snowing.

✖   When you speak with a hushed voice while in your cube, people will assume you're talking to your mother, arranging a job interview, or discussing something x-rated.

✖   Avoid these excuses:
   ⊘ We don't have time. (Since we downsized.)
   ⊘ We don't know how. (Because there's no training.)
   ⊘ We tried that before. (Under the last manager.)
   ⊘ We don't have the data. (The systems don't work.)
   ⊘ We're unique. (It's not true.)

✖   Memos with the heading "Expense Report Preparation" never reduce work or expense and are always the source of jokes for employees.

✖   If you have nothing to say, say nothing. You will command much more attention when you do have something to say.

✖   Doing a great job often means you'll get more work. Understand this and use it to your advantage.

✖   If God is in the details, sometimes you may also need an even higher authority to answer the question "To what end are we doing all this?"

✖   "Empowered employees" is often an oxymoron. Set your expectations accordingly.

- "The system will be down" is one of the few constants in organizations.

- Most communication problems can be solved with proximity.

- "Touchy feely" is not a good label. If it's been assigned to you, start doing things that are more practical.

- Just like athletes are attracted to winning teams, employees are attracted to winning departments.

- Harassment is an act of misconduct. Do it, and you'll lose your job. It's not whether—it's when.

- Always turn your computer on when you're in the office—even if all it shows are toasters flying by.

- Employees give management more credit for being smart than it may deserve. If they sat in on a few management meetings, they would know the truth.

- Most organizations have about the right number of people—they're just doing the wrong things.

- Read the company newsletter.

- Hope is a required ingredient for success.

✘ Employee turnover can have its virtues.

✘ There is no relationship between morale and organizational success. Positive morale does, however, make showing up for work more enjoyable.

✘ New hires should bring new perspectives, not the company line.

✘ The golden rule at work should be: Employees should feel a sense of reward and recognition equal to or greater than their contributions.

✘ Never hire a friend. (There are exceptions.)

✘ Never go into a partnership with a friend. (There are exceptions.)

✘ If someone says you're not strategic, try to figure out what that means.

✘ Employees have a need to vent. Let E-mail play the role or hire consultants to make sure employees get that opportunity.

✘ Perks like company-sponsored daycare and workout facilities are never to be taken for granted. As soon as they are, they'll be taken away.

✖   Don't give out your home number unless you want people to call you. If colleagues do call and it's not a good time, tell them so.

✖   A benchmarking visit is not a class trip at the company's expense. It has a purpose and is a measurable activity. Don't make it soft.

✖   Best practices are often confused with soft benchmarking. Know what the difference is.

✖   If you work in a consumer product company, expect your circle of family and friends to grow during the holidays.

✖   If you're going through a divorce, it's probably a good idea to tell your supervisor. You don't need to keep it a secret from others, but you shouldn't use it as an excuse either. Most people don't care if you're single or married. They just want you to be happy.

✖   Let arguments at work die. It's usually not worth it.

✖   Never sit in the dunk tank at the company picnic.

✖   An abundance of worker's compensation issues either means people are getting hurt or people don't want to go back—or both.

✖   Employees don't need incentives to work safely.

- Being asked to work more hours while pay levels stay flat or go down is a deadly combination.

- Listen to field people. They are the most likely to tell the truth.

- Telling ethnic or gay/lesbian jokes or broadcasting on the Web may not get you fired, but it could. At the very least, you'll be labeled something that will hurt your career. Don't do it.

- Be wary of those whose hair is never mussed up.

- Your personal life will always suffer if things are not going well at work. Minimize that impact.

- Go to the company picnic—but don't stay long.

- In outdoor team-building exercises, don't let your team pull your jeans down while using you as a ladder to climb over the "wall."

- Suspenders, bow ties, short skirts, cowboy boots, and big jewelry will always attract attention. Don't wear them if you don't want attention.

- Be nice to receptionists—they can help you. If they don't like you, they can hurt you.

- Never let your guard down around superiors—even when traveling or socializing.

- Get to know the people in the public relations department. They talk to the leadership.

- Don't hang your diplomas in your office unless you're an MD.

- Assume no one can/will keep a secret.

- Don't try to be close friends with subordinates.

- Never go to more than two meetings a day or you will never get anything done.

- You can have fun nearly every day if you approach work with the right attitude.

- It may not be a small world, but there is a small number of people who count.

- Learn to recognize people who are bad medicine and stay away from them.

- Never underestimate the ability of people to develop strange interpretations of anything you write, say, or do.

- Understanding how pay is administered and how decisions are made could save some heartache at raise time.

- Don't sell anything in the office, even Girl Scout cookies.

- Be direct but not confrontational.

- Support recycling. Avoid wasting paper.

- There are work clothes, school clothes, and church clothes. Don't mix them up. The focus at work should be the organization, not your socks.

- All employees—including management—want to know three things when they show up for work: What's my job? How am I doing? and How does my contribution help serve the organization's mission?

- Written visions, missions, and goals are not as important as knowing what you're supposed to do when you show up in the morning.

- When there are tons of sarcastic, cynical cartoons and caricatures in everyone's cubes and offices, there is a problem.

- The word *we* is much more powerful than the word *they*. Too many "theys" make for a victimized organization. "They" usually don't know who they are.

- Self-directed work teams require lots of direction.

- Mushroom management—when employees are kept in the dark and fed bullshit—never works. Employees are very apt at guessing the truth.

- Put the big vertical metal file cabinets in the common areas, not in your office. Better yet, put them on your hard drive.

- Never preface a sentence with the phrase, "I'm not prejudiced, but ..."

- If you're dating someone in the office, don't expect people to talk to you about it. Do expect them to talk to each other about it.

- There are very few places where you can get away with wearing a Hawaiian shirt.

- Think twice before you allow your photo to be taken for a company publication while you're holding a drink.

- Be creative in sending corporate gifts. Everyone already has the Lucite cubes and Plexiglas quartz clocks. Give away wine, old insulators, or fishing reels instead.

- No one should be interested in your sex life. Don't discuss it at work.

- Diversity initiatives are not methods to meet quotas. They are a means to increase productivity.

- "Time-outs" will almost get a child's attention. Think of the corollary that would apply in your work setting.

- Never do anything at any company-sponsored event that you don't want photographed and displayed on the bulletin board on Monday. Be alert for digital cameras.

- Smelling popcorn cooking in the office is a sign that it's time to take a break. A group will form somewhere and follow the smell.

- Don't get too attached to your office or cube and don't spend a great deal of time decorating it. Chances are good that you'll end up sharing it anyway.

- Breakfast meetings are often very effective because there are fewer distractions. There is not much else to do and people don't feel guilty for what they should have been doing. The price is getting up early.

✗   If you call in sick, don't expect anyone to believe that you really are ill.

✗   Keep a *Rand McNally Road Atlas* at work. It will help you know where you're going, know where other people are, or plan your escape.

✗   Be prepared to be fired if you take anything that remotely resembles a weapon to work.

✗   If you think you need a weapon at work—QUIT.

✗   Nothing kills morale faster than politics and favoritism.

✗   There is no reason good enough not to wear comfortable shoes at work.

✗   When working out of your home, get up and take a shower or put your makeup on as if you were about to go somewhere. You'll be productive faster.

✗   There is a direct relationship: The more time you spend decorating your office or cube, the more often you will be moved.

✗   On the Friday afternoon preceding a three-day weekend, expect to be the only one working.

✗   Acting like the smartest person in the room can get you in trouble. Especially if you're not.

✷ How to tell when it is time to go home:
- ◇ You realize that the reason it's so dark is because your eyes are closed.
- ◇ You accidentally erase your only copy of the document that took twenty hours to develop.
- ◇ Your colleagues tell you it's time for a shower.
- ◇ When you call home a strange man (or woman) answers the phone.
- ◇ When day-old take-out food smells good.

✷ Always tell the truth to employees and your boss. It's easier to remember what you said.

✷ When someone says, "Don't worry; you're young and marketable and willing to relocate," it's time to worry.

✷ The grapevine is usually about 90 percent right.

✷ When you interview someone who will be a colleague, two key questions are:
- ◇ Would I want to have dinner with this person (meaning are you willing to spend time with the person)?
- ◇ Would I introduce this person to my mom (meaning are you proud to be affiliated with the person)?

✷ Learn how to conduct an interview so that you get the information you want.

✗   Get people's attention occasionally by doing something that is out of character. Don't be 100 percent predictable.

✗   Use exclamation points in business writing or titles only if someone's life is in danger. Avoid labels such as "The you in marketing!"

✗   The goal is not to be busy. The goal is to contribute something of worth that will make you glow.

✗   Learn what these sayings mean:
  ○ Outside the box.
  ○ No cookie-cutter solution.
  ○ Connect the dots.
  ○ Deep yogurt.

✗   Worry about the big things, and the little things will fall into place—only if you worry about the little things too.

✗   Always play the good cop.

✗   It's rarely a good sign when you don't hear. No news is not good news in sales, consulting, or interviewing.

✗   Don't put anything in your briefcase that you don't want others to see.

✶ Don't steal. Taking office supplies home is stealing. Copying software without permission is stealing.

✶ Guaranteed team meals for late-night sustenance:
- ⊘ Greasy pizza
- ⊘ Cold Chinese take-out
- ⊘ Greasy pizza with veggies
- ⊘ Doughnuts (for the very late nights)
- ⊘ Greasy pizza with thick crusts
- ⊘ Pizza crusts

✶ The test of communications is whether or not employees know what's important.

✶ If you're given the option of confronting someone with an issue that's driving you crazy or letting it fester, confront the person.

✶ If people won't work with you, or you never get picked for projects, you had better ask why. People learn valuable lessons when choosing up sides on the playground.

✶ If you throw a company or departmental party and no one comes, you have a morale or teamwork problem.

✶ Don't show any signs of vanity even if you are vain. A mirror in the cubicle is always in poor taste.

- If there's not a strategy, it can't be implemented.

- Adding more systems to a bad system makes a big bad system.

- "This is a gray area" means we don't know, but we're hoping the other department will handle it.

- Changing the work area always gets attention—good or bad.

-

When you hear…	It could mean…
Strategic consulting	Eliminate corporate staff and decentralize the business.
Benefits choices	It's going to be more expensive with a higher deductible.
Get employees involved	Hold an employee meeting to tell them what is going to happen to them.

- Be sure you have some talent before you volunteer for the company talent show.

- If you're in a tense business situation, ask yourself, "What would Stephen Colbert do?"

- Don't expect people to be 100 percent candid when the protagonists are present. Third parties always become the messengers.

- If you see your name on a yellow stickie on a conference room wall, something very good or very bad is about to happen to you. Find out.

- Be available. It doesn't matter that you have an open-door policy if no one can find you.

- When "hoteling" starts at the office, consider setting up a home office.

- Wave to window washers when they are suspended outside your office window.

- Employee Activity Committees never have enough money and never make employees very active or more satisfied.

- Employees always respond well to initiatives that will truly help the customer.

- When a company cuts costs, those dollars are rarely allocated for employee raises or bonuses. Set your expectations.

- Signing up to do something that you and everyone else know you won't do is a test. If you don't do it and nothing happens, you win. If you don't do it and you get fired, you lose.

- In some memos, the only thing that matters is the CCs.

- Being a voice from the trenches should not give you trench mouth.

- "Narrow to one" means everyone knows what the ultimate decision will be.

- Setting expectations is the most important part of a project.

- In a cover-your-ass environment, the most important work is usually not done.

- The phrase "line of sight" means people can see how their efforts might help achieve results. Employee morale is directly related to line of sight.

- Sometimes in the middle of layoffs and big changes, everyone deserves to be depressed.

- Catching up is hard to do on the job. Spend the extra hours needed to be caught up.

- If your neighbor at work hates you, there's a fifty-fifty chance that you're a bad neighbor.

- Downloading pornographic/offensive materials from the Internet onto your work computer will get you fired. And you will get caught.

- If any of the following is your work nickname, don't expect to get promoted:
  - Sleepy
  - Dopey
  - Clueless
  - The Wicked Witch
  - Goofy
  - Butthead
  - Homer
  - Gomer

- If any of the following is your work nickname, expect to get all of the special projects:
  - Rambo
  - Steamroller
  - Arnold
  - Bulldog
  - ZoomZoom
  - Loose Cannon

- Watch out for people with the following nicknames:
  - Stinky
  - Mr. Burns
  - Hannibal
  - Flanders
  - Loon (for lunatic)
  - Archie Bunker

- The level of attention day-to-day requires is always underestimated.

- Cobbler's children rules usually apply to companies. Information companies are poor at distributing information; PR firms are bad at getting their names known.

- Low cubicle walls don't ensure low organizational walls.

- Someone does read employee surveys. Go ahead and attach those additional pages to express your thoughts.

- Never look over the top of people's cubicles. It is impolite, and you are intruding into their space.

- Standard operating procedures usually are not. Learn how things really get done.

- If you yell at your coworkers constantly, they will get back at you.

- Always know who's "got your back" at work.

- There are hunters, skinners, and farmers at work. Golfers are not part of the equation.

- The line outside the door is always a sign that something really good or really bad is about to happen.

- The more time the company spends on budget preparation, the less useful it will be. Just learn how to do it and get it in.

- Expand your casual dress wardrobe. The number of days you'll be casual will expand.

- "We're asking you to take a pay cut" is not really a question.

- Wearing a sticky paper label with VISITOR on it makes a guest feel like a tourist. If you require visitor badges, make them professional.

- Monthly reports are read 10 percent of the time, at most.

- Plans should never be all numbers.

- Some things won't get fixed until the Band-Aid is ripped off.

- Crisis management over a long period of time is not management.

- If you're not there, expect the work to pile up.

- Categorizing lots of problems into simple buckets makes it seem like there are not as many.

- Go to bat to get your company to contribute to a worthy not-for-profit organization. Even if it seems futile, you'll feel better.

- The answer to any business issue is never "All we are is dust in the wind."

- Preparing budgets and anything related to them is a necessary evil but not a good use of anyone's time or energy.

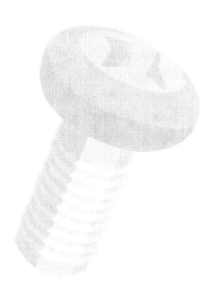

Root Canals and Performance Reviews

It is a rare, very rare performance review system that works. In fact, after working with hundreds of companies, I am not sure I've ever seen one that really measures what you did last year and sets goals for the new year. One thing that performance reviews do is induce a sense of dread and stress.

The reviewer is the one with the keen sense of dread. The reviewer knows that pretty much no matter how self-aware the reviewee is, he or she always believes he or she deserves a higher rating. When I had to do bunches of reviews, I would throw off the reviewee by opening the meeting with something like, "I am happy to say I finished your review, but remind me, is it a 1 that stands for outstanding or a 5?" It would so disarm my charge that when we finally settled on a 3, there was real relief. Most reviews end up at the midpoint anyway—it is a good compromise.

Some organizations try to separate the discussion of performance from the discussion of pay. To the reviewee, this is like separating the jelly from the doughnut, the bumble from the bee. What each of us wants to know in a review is how my efforts convert to cash, as in, "I worked my ass off all year so show me the money and it better be more than Tyrone in the cube next to mine who spent all year talking to his mother about his health problems." Since the reviewer knows he can rarely meet the expectations of the reviewee and he is worried that the reviewee will quit or show up with a gun, the review is a certain source of dread.

For the reviewee, that "special one hour" with the boss to discuss accomplishments and plans is a source of extreme stress. It is an automatic. It is like going to the dentist after you felt a slight twinge in your teeth. Even before that special time with the boss, there is stress based on questions you ask and answer for yourself, like, "Does he/she really know what the hell I did all year? I doubt it." Or, "Was I way too hard on myself in that self-review? I should have given myself more credit." Or, "Should I bring up the fact that I know my boss cheats on his expense reports if he gives me a bad review? Probably not."

The review is stressful even if the evaluation is good. I once had a boss tell me, "We both know you did a great job this year, so in this meeting, let me focus on where you need improvement." Even though I received the highest rating for the hour, I felt that he yelled at me for what a screw-up I was. Total stress.

The actual hour spent with the reviewer is rarely an hour and feels like a parent-teacher conference. Except we are not talking about Sarah who is in the first grade; we are talking about me and what I did and didn't do during the year. By the end, you may be thinking, "Just get me out of here; I don't care what I receive." Like going to the dentist, at the end: "I don't care if you yell at me for not flossing enough; just get me out of here."

The performance review is a perfect storm of both dread and stress. In the end, when the reviewer delivers that 3, both are relieved that it is over for the year and everyone can get back to real work.

⚒ The word *whatever* is properly used in the phrase "Whatever it takes," never as in "Whatever!"

⚒ When someone says, "We need to level set on this," it means someone is about to get his or her expectations brutally corrected.

⚒ A strategy should not be a list of action items that rapidly decompose if anything changes, like the passage of time.

✗   Process escalation means the number of deliverables expected will increase exponentially the closer you get to the due date.

✗   Plan for performance reviews. Know what the measures will be and keep track of them. If you don't know what they are, make them up.

✗   Be prepared for performance reviews—do your own review in advance and give it to your boss.

✗   Always make a self-evaluation of performance very positive.

✗   If you get a bad review, be sure you understand what genuinely needs to be improved upon, as opposed to your boss's perception of how bad things are.

✗   Keep any and all thank-you notes from customers and present them at review time. You won't remember what you accomplished unless you keep some kind of record.

✗   A sigh can often be the key indicator as to whether or not the work will get done and its quality.

✗   Responding to "Requests for Proposals" is not as bad as everyone tells you but worse than you think.

- The fear of someone chasing you is not a good one.

- The fear of someone trying to pass you is not an altogether bad one. It could make you exceed your goals and keep you on your toes.

- Putting parentheses around numbers is a sure way to attract attention.

- Setting expectations with people is the most important part of business. That includes employees, customers, clients, suppliers, consultants, analysts, media, Wall Street, and anyone else. The lesson we can all learn from Southwest Airlines is not about turn times and morale, it is about how well they set expectations.

- "Agree in concept" is usually a long way from "I agree."

- Everything is always SOLD until it is time to collect.

- In your performance review, if the phrase "sets low standards and consistently fails to meet them" appears, look for another job.

- Just because a vision is not clearly communicated doesn't mean one doesn't exist.

- If people say you are working in the white space, they probably don't know what you do.

- Two words to carefully listen for in a performance review are *but* and *however.*

- Even with mature products and processes, look for simple ideas that make for dramatic improvements, like the cardboard sleeve for the cups at Starbucks.

- Being known for having broad bandwidth is a compliment. It has nothing to do with your sex or weight.

- The plastic thingy that holds a six-pack is a good metaphor for pulling a project together.

- ALWAYS spell check, then read it again. A spelling error is a spelling error, no matter where it occurs. They are always noticed.

- Know how to give perfect directions to your home or office.

- Be wary of those who call and say they have no agenda.

- Performance evaluations reflect the organization's attitudes toward employees. Ones that start with attendance and punctuality tell people to show up on time but not necessarily to perform.

- Never confuse making people happy with what needs to be done.

�֎   If you're going to fail, do it fast—but have a recovery strategy.

✖   Progress is made when the choices that are presented are limited and clearly defined. Remember how you deal with your children. Go to bed or take a bath and go to bed. Pick one.

✖   If work goals and criteria for success are not clear, everyone will guess.

✖   Keep a running record of the good things you do throughout the year. Your boss will keep the record of the not-so-good things.

✖   If you get a below-average rating for a reason unclear to you, change departments, change supervisors, or change jobs.

✖   In evaluations, no matter how many numbers there are and what each is supposed to mean regarding competence, if your ranking is in the middle, it means average.

✖   No matter how thoughtful it may be, what everyone looks for in their review is the salary-increase percentage.

✖   Fill out review forms carefully and spend the time necessary to let people know how they are doing.

After a review, everyone should know how they're doing and what else needs to happen. They should not leave dazed and confused.

✗ At some point during each day, lean back in your chair and ask yourself, "What am I doing: is it a high priority, and is it helping me reach my goals?"

✗ Know when you're in batch mode instead of in parallel processing. If so, finish one project before you start another. The world operates in parallel process mode, so it may be hard to be the only batcher around.

✗ If a performance measure is hard to understand, it's not a good one. Use ratios whenever possible in creating measures such as revenues per employee, staff resources compared to line resources, and the like.

✗ One measure is usually not enough. Measures that form equations are the best, like x/y-q/s=effectiveness.

✗ If pushed into recommendations, it's best to create alternatives and let the client choose. Don't be afraid to let your own bias be known, but share the decision-making responsibility. Always share the blame.

✖   Work plans are useful only if they're short and include names, times, and outcomes.

✖   If you don't have a client or customer, find one—before you have to find a job.

✖   Performance measures should be viewed liked the instruments on a car. It's a complementary set that tells you how you're doing. None really stands alone.

✖   Performance review systems rarely work. If you need to do reviews, create your own system that fits.

✖   Learn the difference between running a meeting and leading a group.

✖   Spend five minutes figuring out how to communicate the decision for every ten minutes you spend deciding.

✖   Data is not inherently good or bad, but accurate data that drives decisions quickly is good.

✖   Occasionally ask yourself, "If I had to bill my time, would anyone pay for it?"

✖   There is no such thing as a probationary period. We're all on probation, every day.

✖   We all know how we do in job interviews, sales calls, and meetings. Reconcile your expectations accordingly.

✗ When everyone "games" the numbers, change the measurement system to change the games.

✗ Always know who your client or customer is—no matter what your job is.

✗ De facto means no one ever made the decision but now we're stuck with it. Revisit those decisions.

✗ When waiting in a lobby for a meeting or to meet someone, don't sit down.

✗ Keep track of what you do—someone is sure to ask.

✗ Get out of the office as much as you can—especially if you're with clients or customers.

✗ Make decisions in a timely fashion, even if you're not 100 percent certain that it's the right decision. Not deciding is a decision too.

✗ Making a decision and doing something is better than doing nothing—no matter the size of the decision.

✗ Ask for input only if you plan to do something with it and about it.

✗   Avoid the "Abilene Paradox" where everyone does something that no one wants to do because no one could make up their mind.

✗   Learn to be a sponge. Observe everything and everyone around you. The information will come in handy later.

✗   Create a logic to any decisions you make, at least in your own mind.

✗   Share the credit for successful projects and make sure everyone's supervisor knows of everyone's contribution.

✗   Focus on the most important things to do to help your department or organization be successful. Don't focus on the easiest things.

✗   Treat your time as if someone is paying for it—someone is.

✗   If you're going to complain about something, have a solution in mind and make clear what you want.

✗   Long hours don't mean anything—results count, not effort.

- Rejoice in the successful completion of projects and major activities. Remember how it felt to put that calculus text away, knowing you'd never have to open it again.

- Develop a point of view about success—your own and your organization's.

- Read your job description but never be restricted by it. Do what needs to be done.

- If your desk faces the door, don't look up every time someone passes.

- Always know how you perform—be honest with yourself and do better next time.

- If you're in a focus group, make sure you can trust everyone before you speak your mind.

- Don't take sick days unless you are sick.

- Spend your department's budget as if it were your own.

- Leave your office building at least once every day, even if it's January and you work in Anchorage. It will clear your head.

- Never apologize for an idea that didn't work—but always admit a mistake.
- A good source of names for initiatives and speeches is country-western album covers.
- Learn what finished work looks like and then deliver your own work only when it looks the same way.
- The age of strategic planning is over…it is now the age of implementation.
- Always ask, "Why are we doing this?" before proceeding.
- Remember that almost all business is painfully simple. Strive to demystify.
- Don't confuse extensive documentation of a situation with insight, and don't confuse spreadsheets with analysis.
- Don't get hung up defining whether you're working on a vision or a mission or goals or objectives—do what's important.
- If you're put in a spot where you are the process consultant, keep the meeting moving and know your audience.

- The best mission statement ever written is that of Federal Express: To deliver the package the very next morning, regardless.

- Beware of a false sense of activity—e.g., you're too busy to go to the bathroom but you're not sure what all of your work will add up to.

- Action follows intent. If you intend to lose weight, act like you're on a diet. If you intend to be customer- or quality-driven, act that way.

- If you are placed on a Total Quality team, do something worthwhile; don't redesign forms.

- Performance evaluations take place every day, not every six months or every year.

- Focus on what peers and supervisors will remember.

- Past performance is the best indicator of future performance. Remember this whenever a leopard claims to have changed its spots.

- Fear is not a good motivator. It only works in the short term.

- Measures that penalize people don't work. The penalties are less important than the measures.

- Don't complain about "deadwood." Figure out ways to get rid of it. The deadwood always know who they are.

- Allocate more time for any job than you think it will take. Twice as much is not a bad start.

- Work "without a net." Don't build systems or organizations around something that has never happened—unless you're NASA. Take risks.

- The only thing that's read in most reports is the executive summary. Make sure that section really tells the story with a beginning, middle, and end.

- "Good ol' boy" systems should always be replaced by performance-based systems. Good ol' boys can be anyone.

- If Employee of the Month systems work, why is that parking space always empty?

- Never assume people will understand acronyms. Acronyms will always make you sound like a geek or a big company guy.

- Sending too many messages to your children or employees means they won't know what to do.

✷   The opposite of gridlock is risk taking. When things are getting stuck, increase your willingness to take risks.

✷   If you ask for feedback don't expect to hear what you want.

✷   If you raise expectations, performance needs to be raised too.

✷   Notice what others at your level think they're too good to do and learn it well. You'll get the reputation as someone who gets the job done.

✷   The fear of being average is a powerful motivator for ambitious people. Listen to that fear if it's bubbling up.

✷   Overnight successes don't exist.

✷   The vast majority of articles written about any organization are accurate. Business journalists don't make things up.

✷   When you hear, "With all we've been through together," it means you are about to get to a deeper level of friendship with someone—or get fired.

✷   Know what "extremely urgent" means. Usually, unless there's blood or money involved, it's not that important.

- Having both standards and flexibility can be done. It's just not easy.

- Describe your job as if it's the most interesting one in the world—even if it's not.

- Being too busy with no time to think is the common denominator of work. Adjust the numerator so the equation works for you.

- VSOP (Visible Signs of Progress) is often more important than million-dollar strategy reports.

- Fantasies and reunions are great motivators.

- Always create a flurry of activity three months before performance-review time. It will be fresh in your supervisor's mind.

- "If we had the time, we could do it the right way" is a poor excuse for bad work. There is no good excuse for bad work. There is always a way to find more time somewhere. Look in the "cancelled meetings" closet.

- A whistle and clipboard will often put you in charge.

- Spend five minutes occasionally just reflecting on what you're spending your time doing and ask yourself if you've become exactly what you thought you never would.

✖   One measure of productivity is not paying for what no one is doing.

✖   Big fires from little fires grow. If there are a bunch of little things wrong that never get fixed, they will eventually kill all progress.

✖   In a sales situation, give the impression that you love what you do.

✖   Never get in contests with others about who is working hardest. It's not a contest you want to win.

✖   Being direct may catch people off-guard, but they almost always appreciate it.

✖   When communication is cited as the big problem, it usually means no one believes it, not no one is talking.

✖   If you lose one button on a button-down shirt, buy a new shirt.

✖   Rotating bald tires is a huge activity that changes nothing. It's a good metaphor by which to measure your own activities.

✖   If your performance review is the same year after year, you either have a very boring job or no one is doing your review.

✷   People who believe they are empowered will do more than the company expects if they have any idea what the company expects.

✷   Progress and improvements are made day to day, not year to year.

✷   Fight feelings of entitlement. Feeling entitled will not motivate you to perform or help you get what you want and deserve.

✷   When someone in the systems group tells you that "you can have it good, fast, or cheap—pick any two," pick two and hold them to it.

✷   Empowerment means you can sign off on something even if it's little.

✷   When faced with difficult decisions or tight deadlines, ask yourself, "What's the worst that can happen if...?" The answer is usually not as bad as you feared.

✷   Never take calculus, chemistry, and accounting in the same semester. Never take on projects at work that remind you of the time you took those three classes at the same time.

✷   Read the business and trade publications—especially *BusinessWeek*, *Fortune*, and the *Wall Street Journal*—so you understand trends and know buzzwords.

�֎   How to tell when you're in trouble with either vendors or procurement people, depending on which side you are on:

⊘   All words that you previously agreed upon look suspiciously different.

⊘   You catch the "other side" doing the Nerd Dance after you leave.

⊘   The other side knows your position and numbers better than you do.

⊘   A photo of your face is seen on dartboards in cubes.

✖   Don't promise what you can't deliver.

✖   Remember that the purpose of business is to make or do something and sell it. The closer you can get to those activities, the better.

✖   If you're in a staff job, get line experience by jumping at assignments out in the trenches.

✖   Take a time-management course and then develop your own system that will work.

✖   As tedious as it may be, understand your health benefits and keep track of them.

✖   Maintain a sense of humor and inject it when appropriate.

✖   Learn to read financial statements.

- Know how to write business letters and send them—including thank-you letters and proposal letters.

- Develop a high tolerance for ambiguity—you'll be more satisfied.

- Learn to remember people's names. If your memory is poor, develop a system.

- Learn how to give first-rate presentations so that the message you're trying to deliver is the same one the audience receives.

- Be comfortable around senior managers, or learn to fake it.

- Understand the skills and abilities that differentiate you from everyone else. Whenever you have the opportunity, use them.

- At minimum, learn how to use a spreadsheet software program and PowerPoint.

- Learn how to run a meeting well, and learn how to prepare a good meeting agenda.

- Know the perceptions people have of you. If people see you as "a whiner" or "too political," change that perception.

✖   When giving a talk or a presentation, always consider what thought you want the audience to walk away with.

✖   Get at least one article published per year that will garner recognition in your field.

✖   Create a great opening to speeches and presentations; use it often or until you get sick of it.

✖   A little self-effacing humor can be an effective icebreaker; just don't use too much.

✖   If you don't know the answer, say so.

✖   Take a counseling course and develop a "bedside manner" for dealing with clients and associates.

✖   Give presentations that tell stories, not just provide data.

✖   Become proficient in another language—or at least get the tapes and try.

✖   Go through an Outward Bound course. It shouldn't be on-the-job.

✖   Take risks with your ideas and with implementing them.

✖   Use metaphors to convey your point.

- Being good is important; being trusted is essential.

- Become known for building ideas, not finding fault.

- Although everyone hates it, understand the budgeting process and what it means to your group.

- Big investments in small projects rarely lead to big projects. There is no relationship between the investment and the results.

- Learn the difference between Theory X and Theory Y and Type A and Type B and the definition of the Hawthorne Effect.

- Reduce an analysis to three bullet points; no one will take the time to understand, pay attention to, or remember any more.

- Skimming and cherry picking sound like farmer terms but dictate very different marketing approaches.

- Strive to be an "impact player"—i.e., someone who makes a difference no matter what the situation.

- Like they say in boxing, "Always finish stronger than you start." People remember the end of the project.

- The old model said that managers didn't do anything but "manage"; the new rules say that managers must do.

- Trust is as important as competence and more important than affinity.

- If trust as a value requires verification, there's a lot of work to do.

- Sometimes saying nothing and waiting until the other side makes a move is the best offense.

- Boil down your job far enough so that you can describe it to anyone easily.

- Be honest with yourself about your strengths and weaknesses and manage accordingly.

- Stay with something long enough to learn and make a contribution.

- Don't create reports that sit on shelves. Reports should be a means to an operational end.

- Don't get a reputation for being a climber or a political animal; get a reputation for always doing what is right.

- Being in the right place at the right time is never an accident.

- Teamwork will become more and more important. Learn what it is and how to be a good team member.

- Know when you are at your best—morning, night, under pressure, relaxed—and schedule and prioritize work accordingly.

- Don't be a process consultant without having some content knowledge as well.

- Learn what the differences are between marketing, sales, public relations, and advertising.

- There is a marketing element to everything you do in any organization.

- Understanding the difference between what the organization says and what it does will help focus on basic problems.

- The best thing about training is the people you meet in your class.

- If you learn and apply even one idea from a training session, it has been worthwhile.

- Before you get retrained for a new job, make certain of where the retraining will get you and that you'll learn something new.

✖ Training is often seen as a reward and a sign that the organization is willing to invest in you. Take advantage of it but be realistic about what you will really learn.

✖ Don't expect that things will be different back at the ranch after you finish a training program.

✖ The best training is provided by your customers.

✖ Take a good presentation skills class.

✖ Learn how to stand up in front of a room and take notes at the same time.

✖ Learn to listen to clients, customers, and employees and base your actions on what you hear. If people on your team are not good listeners, interpret for them until they become good listeners.

✖ Guessing between the essential, the critical, and the absolutely necessary is how most people spend their time on the job. The shades of difference could make the difference between success and failure.

✖ Most work activities are neither essential, critical, nor absolutely necessary. They still need to be done every day.

- Become familiar with the systems and people at the neighborhood Kinko's and other copy/computer/printer facilities. These places can save your life when faced with a deadline. If you're on a deadline and not familiar with the system, take someone who is.

- Don't answer your own questions, especially if they are part of an evaluation. It rarely pays well to say, "Were my expectations met? I don't think so."

- Employees will continue to be asked to do more with the same resources—or with even less. Get used to it.

- Sometimes there are no alternatives to practice and experience.

- Don't use the letters *i.e.* in speaking.

- Nothing tells more about what you think is important than your schedule.

Where Are the Doughnuts?

There are just too many meetings. They have taken over our lives. People barely get their "real work" done between meetings, voice mails, and E-mails. I know a lot of people who attend meetings with a chip on their shoulder because the price they pay for too many meetings is working late or on weekends—away from their families.

Everyone underestimates how long meetings will take. The concept of "hard stop" dictates meetings must end at a certain time. It's rare that hard stops work. It's more likely people just get up and leave with the meeting still going on. There is also always the risk of the ten- or fifteen-minute remainder talk in the hall, where some of the decisions are actually made. If meetings have become the alternative to work, PowerPoint presentations have become the alternative to thinking in meetings. Clues it will be a bad meeting include when someone shows up with big spreadsheets or thirty slides for a forty-five-minute meeting.

Too many meetings was once a vice; now it is a bad habit. The attitude is, It's Friday at ten, it must be time for that meeting, whether we need it or not. There are, of course, exceptions, based on the industry. In the airline business, for instance, crew meetings before takeoff are a good idea.

Meetings always go at least as long as you have scheduled. Show me a meeting that ends early and I'll show you a bunch of happy people. Unfortunately, early ending meetings are a sign of an empty agenda or disengaged participants, not efficiency and focus. "Let's try to finish this meeting early" is one of the great lies of today.

Some meetings divide responsibility and blame into such small parts that no one has any real accountability. Writing on the white board or giving a PowerPoint presentation does not necessarily equate with getting something done.

Meetings are seen as the only way to communicate, even though E-mail has become a more effective and efficient communications tool. In meetings, we typically spend the time telling people what they already know.

Many people are worried about their jobs, and they equate talking in meetings with class participation—as in, "Maybe I'll get extra credit if I ask a question that will make my boss look good," even though everyone already knows the answer. A meeting can also be called without a clear sense of purpose. If the outcome of a meeting is to schedule another meeting, it was probably not a good meeting.

Details dominate meetings. Most meetings drown in a level of detail that is not necessary to achieve the desired outcome. There is so much data available that everyone has learned the fastest way to derail a meeting is to go down deep into the details. Once derailed, there may not be time to do the presentation you didn't prepare.

Draining E-mail or talking on a cell phone in the hall is not being present at a meeting. I was invited to a meeting where the host was pounding out instant messages during the entire meeting. It was not only offensive, but made me wonder, Why bother to have the meeting?

New Year's resolutions include: lose weight, exercise more, read more, and the new one that's entered the list of promises we can't keep: attend fewer meetings. Meetings keep getting scheduled, and we keep going in spite of our best-intended resolutions.

Telling the truth means discussing what is most pressing and being direct with everyone in the meeting in order to move things forward. Meetings where the truth is not told are placeholders for the next meeting. If truth and presence dominated all meetings, it would be a better world.

- Never go to more than two meetings a day.
- Never call a meeting before 7 a.m. or after 6 p.m.
- Tell the truth in meetings. If the project is off track, say so.

- Use meetings to communicate. What you meet about tells the organization what is important.

- Don't set up meeting rules that you know you can't keep. The biggest offending rule is "We will start on time no matter who is here."

- Don't make people late for their next meeting. If you promised to get out at 2:00, do it.

- Don't fall asleep or make your grocery list in meetings. People do notice.

- Discuss what is most important. Don't ignore what everyone really wants to discuss.

- Never waste people's time. They will be mad and won't show up next time.

- Avoid "touchy, feely" at all costs. "How is everyone feeling?" is not a good question when discussing business results. Plus, you may hear things you really didn't want to hear.

- Pretend to be smart, even when you're clueless.

- Don't gossip in meetings. Don't do things that make you a party to gossip or the subject of gossip.

✷   Figure out what you want to communicate after every meeting. If you've nothing to say, figure out why you met.

✷   Never, ever wordsmith in a meeting. If you are considering a slogan, tagline, vision, or mission, this is doubly true.

✷   If you leave a meeting talking to yourself, you didn't have a good meeting; don't call another one. Get it done in a different way.

✷   Serve refreshments or at least allow people to show up with their own coffee.

✷   Take breaks when you say you will so people can set their restroom expectations.

✷   Evaluate meetings. Keep the ones that you need and change the ones that you don't.

✷   There are single-function and multi-function breaks. Let people know if it's just the bathroom, just the phones, just the coffee, or all three. All breaks at meetings last longer than they are supposed to.

✷   Don't cancel an appointment five minutes after you're expected. If you were supposed to be there, be there.

- No time is ever good for everyone. The more time you spend trying to find the perfect time, the fewer the people who can attend.

- Some meetings are like listening to a long line of radio commercials only to hear a song that you hate.

- The best meeting facilitator can be Instant Messenger. When participants are pinging each other with messages saying, "Let's get the meeting back on track," or "We're diving into too much detail," or "What the f--- is this guy talking about?" it's time to fix the meeting.

- Remind meeting attendees of what they agreed to by documenting all results.

- The question "Can we do a process check?" means people no longer know why they are there or what they are doing. Pity the meeting leader when you hear it.

- Politics can convert a one-hour meeting into an eight-hour meeting with no result.

- Never put anyone from the legal department on the agenda first. The lawyer will take too long and lose everyone's interest.

- Leading a meeting and facilitating a meeting are not the same.

✻   "Long and wrong" should be a phrase used to describe golf games, not meetings or presentations.

✻   No matter how long the meeting, the good stuff will happen at the end.

✻   When others are on a speakerphone, always know who could be listening on the other end.

✻   The actual presentation time that you will get on stage will always be less than promised.

✻   Food to never eat in your car on the way to a meeting:
     ⊘ Burritos
     ⊘ Whoppers
     ⊘ Big Macs
     ⊘ Leftovers
     ⊘ Jelly doughnuts

✻   All meeting agendas are tentative.

✻   The easiest way to derail a meeting is to ask a question that will require a lot of detail.

✻   Don't roll your eyes in meetings.

✻   When the outcome of a meeting is to have another meeting, it has been a lousy meeting.

✷   Violent agreement often occurs in meetings. Know when it's happening so you can move on.

✷   Always take notes in meetings. Never assume others will, even when they say they will.

✷   Next steps from meetings must always be clear.

✷   If you meet in a resort area, give people time off so they can enjoy it. Don't go to Orlando or Vail and stick people in windowless meeting rooms all day.

✷   Never start out a meeting or a speech with anything remotely resembling "I'm sorry, I have a cold," or "…that we're late," or "…there's a typo."

✷   The final presentation/recommendation should never come as a surprise to the client, task force, or your boss.

✷   Don't be afraid to ask the big question; other people are probably wondering about it too.

✷   Accidental meetings, in the halls or at the coffee wagon, can be more valuable than formal meetings. Circulate.

✷   Never show a chart or diagram that people can't read in a presentation.

- Set up ground rules at planning or decision-making meetings and get everyone to agree. Spell out the behavior that you're after. Some examples are:
  - It's okay to fight, just "don't go to bed mad."
  - Attack issues, not individuals.
  - Stick to the agenda.
  - Think creatively.
  - Work toward solutions and results, not processes.
  - Look toward making things better. Don't dwell in the past.

- If, during a presentation, everyone has left the room, or everyone is talking, take a break.

- Never start a meeting or a retreat with a blank sheet of paper.

- Meetings always seem to last 50 percent longer than you think they will. Plan accordingly.

- Ask for questions only if you have time to answer them.

- During a presentation, there is a direct relationship between lighting and sleeping. The darker the room, the more sleepers. If it doesn't need to be dark, don't make it so. Open the blinds and let light in. Too many meetings are held overlooking beautiful spots with the blinds closed.

- When giving any type of demo in front of a large group, have a backup plan. If the president or major clients are in the room, have a backup plan and a resume.

- If a meeting can't end until someone volunteers to do something, be that volunteer.

- Tell people to hold their questions until the end of a presentation only if you want very few questions or if everyone in the room reports to you.

- If you're giving a presentation, don't stand in the dark or people will think you are in the dark. Find the spotlight, no matter how subtle. Speak from where people will see you.

- Not every meeting or discussion needs to be guided by PowerPoint presentations. They often inhibit useful discussion. "Death by PowerPoint" is a phrase that is too often true. Tell a compelling story with key messages, PowerPoint or not.

- In presentations, know where to point a remote computer mouse. Otherwise it looks like you're trying to contact aliens. Of course, depending on the presentation, you may be looking to aliens for help.

- There should be one slide for every five minutes of talk, not five slides for every one minute of talk. What you don't present will never be seen. Be thankful if what you do present is seen.

- Without the right people in the meeting, there will be more than one meeting.

- The most dreaded words in any presentation are: These numbers don't look right.

- In meetings with lots of people around a table and one person on the speakerphone, talk to each other; don't yell at the phone.

- If you eat like a child—that is, play with your food and eat with your hands—sit in an inconspicuous spot in business meetings where food is served.

- Prioritize all meetings and only go to the really important ones.

- Never try to accomplish more than three things in any one meeting.

- Ask questions at company meetings, but don't embarrass anyone.

- Off-site meetings always have agendas that are way too packed. Plan to be home later than you thought.

✄   The Arc of the Off-Site Planning Session:

⊘ 8:00 – Optimism Phase – The team believes that a clear plan will emerge by noon and the afternoon is for golf and spa treatments.

⊘ 10:00 – Ambition Phase – The team believes that it may not have a complete plan with details but a crisp roadmap could emerge. Willing to commit to the afternoon for completion.

⊘ 12:00 – Lunch is a welcome break.

⊘ 12:30 – Realism Phase - Lunch is cut short in the hopes of completion. Team is still debating the difference between a mission and a vision statement. Small groups sure to follow. Doubts about completion begin to cloud thinking.

⊘ 3:00 – Pessimism Phase – The team completes review of fourth draft of mission statement and begins wordsmithing. Many start checking E-mail and playing with BlackBerry.

⊘ 5:00 – Promissory Phase – Leaders agree that the bulk of the work needs to be done "off-line." Everyone agrees. Where is the cocktail hour?

⊘ 7:00 – Completion Phase – While at the bar the team agrees to stay in touch and work together on no more than five top priorities. The planning meeting is a success.

- When giving a presentation, don't read the slides and don't use a pointer.

- If the result of a meeting is a form, it was a meeting that produced the wrong deliverable.

- When giving presentations, read the audience continuously. Change the tenor, subject, or speaker if you are losing them.

- Always sit at the conference table—never by the wall.

- Constructing a matrix can create a very powerful picture. Use one whenever you can.

- Children are a source of truth and ideas. The icebreaker to use in intense meetings was developed by a six-year-old: "Raise your hand who's mad."

- Using macho sports or military metaphors usually means you've lost half your audience.

- Never put more than twenty words on a presentation page. Use graphics. If you want to lose the audience, show slides with columns of numbers.

- Never go into a meeting without knowing what you want the outcome(s) to be.

- The top ten danger words and red alert phrases to listen for when senior management is giving a State of the Business presentation:
  - Repositioning
  - Transition
  - One time
  - Fine tuning
  - Upgrading
  - Disappointed
  - Not final numbers
  - Adjusting
  - Talent shortage
  - Shortfall

- During a presentation, never say, "I'll get into this in a lot more detail in a minute."

- Never start a presentation by saying, "I know you can't read this, but ..." or "Bear with me while I ..."

- Humor can only go so far if you're ill prepared. If there are typos throughout the presentation, stop joking about them and pointing them out after the second page.

- Borrow David Letterman's "Top 10 List" concept when giving presentations.

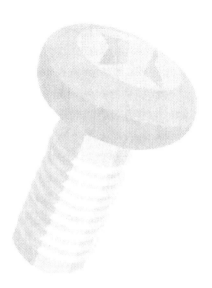

5

Managing - Pushing and Pulling on Ropes

When I once worked with a large bank, one of the employees told me that his department had a yellow-stickie manager. I immediately knew exactly what he meant. His story confirmed my initial reaction.

In this particular department, the manager would respond to every transaction with a small yellow note stuck to the edge of something. Notes would be lined up on the edge of people's desks in the morning and hung on the backs of chairs and on computer screens. The most common message on the notes would be "See me ASAP" or "Who authorized this?!?" There was no need for initials at the bottom of the note; everyone knew who was sending them. And everyone dreaded them. As the employee told me, "It's to the point where we are scared to death of those x*!@%#&! yellow stickies."

There are plenty of things we should all fear in life. Yellow stickies should not be high on the list. At the bank in question, the yellow stickies had become a substitute for effective management—they were a symbol of bad management delivered efficiently.

My intention is to help people recognize that efficiency should not replace effectiveness and that if you are doing stupid things, those around you will notice. How you are perceived and how you respond to all kinds of situations is important and will affect your career.

We are all managers. If we are not managing a department, we are managing our time, our children, or our money. The trick in managing is to find the balance between planning, organizing, controlling, and doing. And most importantly, to know what is most important.

⚒ Note to Donald Trump: Telling people "You're fired!" is never funny. If you've ever heard those words, no doubt, you will agree.

⚒ While on LOA, including maternity, talk to your boss occasionally while you're gone so he or she is not surprised when you come back. If necessary, make up reasons to engage in dialogue. You will learn more about your job and whether or not you even want it back.

⚒ Team-based leaders may be the way of the future, but the hierarchical animals will never be extinct.

- A BFO is a Blinding Flash of the Obvious. Not to be confused with a BFD.

- When you hear comments from executives that sound something like, "I don't know what those people do," those people should start looking for another job.

- If your boss says, "Your job is to make me look good," it probably is.

- Artificial deadlines that make people stay up all night create halfhearted efforts and create big bad voodoo toward the person who created the deadline.

- All candidates for any job need to be sold, no matter how special you believe your organization to be.

- If your boss tells you to consider another line of work or says, "This doesn't seem to be the right fit for you," you are being fired. It may not be your last day, but that is coming soon too.

- It is never worth debating the relative importance of integrity, honesty, and trustworthiness. Be known for them all.

- Poor performers require ten times more time than solid performers.

- Poor performers who are in denial about their performance require fifty times more time.

- If your boss is giving your name out to search consultants, it's probably time to exercise some job-hunting initiatives of your own.

- If you tell your new boss to take a number and get in line because you have so many bosses, the organization is overly matrixed.

- Lucite cubes are better for butterflies and fossils than logos or stock offerings. Save the money and give it to the employees.

- Variety is what everyone wants on the job. Variety can kill efficiency. Get the balance right.

- Just because you're a supervisor doesn't mean you have a license to be a jerk.

- If your span of control is bigger than your shoe size, your job as a manager is probably safe.

- If you think you're smarter than your boss, never let on. Your boss knows anyway.

- Employees who say, "I only get paid to think from the neck down," are in trouble.

- Supervisors who say you only get paid to think from the neck down should be fired.

- Don't try to get even with the organization or the boss. No one will win, but you *will* lose.

- Don't spend a lot of time creating missions—ask your employees what they do.

- When *BusinessWeek*, *Forbes*, or *Fortune* announce a management trend, learn as much as you can about it. It will impress your boss.

- Don't hire only people who look and act like you. It will make for a less interesting and less effective group.

- The most effective suggestion system is the one where the CEO puts a sign over his or her door that says "Suggestion Box."

- Never expect the employees to be truly honest in front of their boss.

- If, in front of your boss, you pull the door when the handle says push, just keep going.

- Never give a bad reference. Simply decline to comment if there's nothing good to say.

- Managing by E-mail is not managing; it's E-mail.

- When someone says they need to see you, it's really important, and will only take five minutes, that person is about to resign.

- If you have to fire someone, it should only be a five-minute meeting. Avoid "This hurts me more than it does you."

- Stop looking for more time and start looking for more ways to use the time you have.

- Surfing the Net for research may be fun, but your boss probably believes it's more like playing video games than doing your job.

- Letting your boss know you're critical of him or her, even in private, could show up on your performance review later.

- Never give people choices you don't really want them to take.

- If you have to fire someone, just do it. Everyone recognizes deadwood, and no one likes it.

- Faces that say "no" all the time mean the answer will almost always be "no."

- When making assignments, the questions should be: Will he/she do it? Will he/she fit? Will he/she know how?

- Yellow stickies left on computer screens at night with cryptic messages are not a substitute for management or communications.

- Morale is hard to change without finding villains and punishing them.

- Morale doesn't necessarily improve when the news for the organization is good.

- Sharing in the misery can be a team-building exercise.

- Know which group function or department is the samurai of your organization.

- Bark at the moon, not your boss.

- Ask a lot of questions about decision making, like: Is there a decision that you want me to make? How do we make a decision on this? When can we expect a decision?

- In any decision-making process there is a finite number of options, usually not more than five. They include: (1) Keeping things the way they are; and (5) Changing everything in a dramatic way. Which really leaves three options. Pick one and move forward.

- Supervisors who think their job is to babysit will be eliminated sooner or later.

- Teams at work should act and perform like basketball teams, not relay teams.

- Teams need goals, resources, clear roles, equipment, and food.

- If you give your boss a ride in your car and he or she asks if you have a dog, because of the smell and the mess, always say yes.

- Telling your boss about your sexploits will always backfire.

- Favoritism will hurt performance and kill morale.

- Spend *almost* all of your budget every year.

- Every clarification of plans or strategies will breed new questions.

- Don't use yellow stickies as a way to threaten people.

- Never assume people know why they showed up. Eighty percent of life may be showing up, but once they are there, 80 percent of success is telling them why they showed up.

- If you don't like the answers you get, try asking different questions. Don't just repeat the same questions to your boss's boss.
- Bean-counter jokes about senior management are rarely funny and say nothing more than someone is minding the financial store.
- Cutting activities like holiday parties or company picnics will knock the wind out of morale, even among those who never planned to attend.
- People stay with organizations because of their coworkers and the challenge.
- International transposition of U.S. ways is not the same as globalization.
- Never confuse a memo with reality ... most memos from the top don't change the work you do.
- Fighting over revenue or expense transfers is a very unproductive use of company time.
- Making it hard to get things done will make high turnover easier to accomplish.
- Delegation means you don't do some of the work anymore. Don't turn delegation into duplication.

- When someone submits his or her resignation, just accept it. Trying to talk someone out of quitting rarely works, in business or in love.

- Remember that everyone laid off is someone's mom or dad or son or daughter.

- Do a practice round before you play golf with your boss or your customer.

- Getting "written up" is the same as hearing "Wait till your father gets home."

- Final pay decisions are often only as good as your boss's presentation skills. Take up a collection to send the boss to presentation-skills training.

- Uneven workloads will kill teamwork.

- The word *shot* should not be used to describe displaced workers.

- Realistic planning is the easiest way to reduce stress and pressure.

- The greatest compliment is "Management does the right things."

- Having a vision doesn't necessarily help with what we're supposed to do next week.

- Phantom stock plans are never understood. No one expects the plan ever to pay out.

- It's okay for a big company to have a small-company attitude. It's not okay for a big company to have small-company systems.

- Sales force incentive systems should be understood by everyone in the company, upside and downside. It's the only way non-salespeople can deal with the trips to Hawaii.

- Schedules are not more important than quality.

- Managing up is not a substitute for managing across and down.

- Growth can hide real deficiencies until you stop growing.

- People don't want to work for a department or a division; they want to work for a company. It's all about pride.

- Incentive plans that don't pay out create no incentives.

- Pace dictates the number of problems and the number of opportunities.

- If you're not on the job, don't expect the supervisor to know how to do your job.

✖   Treating people like numbers will prevent the company from meeting its numbers.

✖   The best examples of process efficiency are usually in the take-out deli. Pay attention at lunch.

✖   At least 50 percent of any project is putting together the to-do list or plan.

✖   Death certificates should never be required if an employee asks for a bereavement day.

✖   Happy workers don't always make good workers, but good workers make for happy workers ... Focus your efforts on getting yourself and others to work well.

✖   Always strive for a deeper level of truth with business associates. Posturing and pretending is always transparent to everyone.

✖   Suggestion systems can work—don't be reluctant to use them.

✖   Don't have anyone on your team whom you wouldn't trust with your kids.

✖   Whenever executives start talking about competition, be prepared for cost reduction.

✖   Always arrive at work thirty minutes before your boss.

✹   The size of your office is not as important as the size of your paycheck.

✹   Don't surround yourself with people who are like you; strive for difference and diversity.

✹   Most autocratic executives are like the man behind the curtain in *The Wizard of Oz*: They are really more human than the wizards they are trying to be.

✹   Work on problems, not symptoms. Morale itself is never a problem; something is happening that causes low morale, which creates a problem.

✹   Don't make people feel bad when they make a mistake.

✹   Read the same book the boss is reading.

✹   Life may not be fair in the short term, but it does even out in the long term. Butthead bosses do "get theirs" in the long term.

✹   Organizations should have one mission that is clearly understood. Everyone may have their own interpretation, but the interpretation should be a variation on the same theme.

✹   If something isn't working, don't put the blame on the mission or vision; it's almost always something else that precludes you from reaching the vision. Most likely, the actions don't support the intent.

✗ If your organization's mission is described as "generic," throw it away and create a new one.

✗ "What's in it for me?" is the wrong question. A better one is, "Is it in my best interest in the long term to...?"

✗ Credibility means people believe you will do it, not people hear what you say.

✗ Abdication of responsibility without a reason will come back to haunt you and probably reduce your job to something less than you want it to be.

✗ Give leaders a chance. Most organizational and policy issues are not solved quickly or without pain. Increments toward a positive end is often the only option.

✗ Organizations have more filters than they have effective communication vehicles. Know what filters the information has been through by the time you receive it.

✗ Leadership is more about communication and credibility than it is about policy and performance.

- Always provide a context to help people understand what is happening.

- Executives with bathrooms in their offices probably don't spend a whole lot of time with employees.

- Apply the lessons from Dr. Seuss's books to your own organization and make policies as simple to understand as his books.

- In a management shake-up, if no one loses their job, it isn't a shake-up.

- When your boss always uses phrases like "in the crosshairs" or "get a bead on them," look for another boss—unless you're in the army.

- There are at least two people you should never offend: your boss's assistant and your boss's spouse. Either could make your life miserable.

- Never complain about a peer's promotion. You will only look petty and jealous. There will always be someone who gets a better deal than you, but your turn will come.

- Most companies know how to cut costs because they've had lots of practice.

✷   "It's the union" is never an appropriate excuse for management or rank file.

✷   Not utilizing the skills of employees is the worst crime of management.

✷   The Magic 8 Ball is not a forecasting tool. "Outlook hazy, try again" should not be an option.

✷   Deadwood on the job should never be tolerated. If you know you're deadwood, quit or retire. If you're surrounded by deadwood that no one will address, change jobs.

✷   Long-shot statements like "The chances of this happening are as good as winning the lottery" sometimes come true. Be careful and not negative.

✷   Standards should be applied. If they're not, they're not standards.

✷   When someone resigns and then changes his or her mind, start looking for a replacement. It's only a matter of time before he or she resigns again.

✷   Don't go on *Oprah* or any talk show when they're talking about Bosses from Hell unless you've just won the lottery.

- If work isn't getting done, reprimands are rarely the answer.

- Managers more concerned with power and ego than productivity have employees who are destined to fail. It just may take a while.

- The fastest way to solve the problem of too many meetings may be to change the role of the middle managers.

- No one should come to work and have to walk on eggs. It would be better to walk the people creating this environment out the door.

- Good managers always know the real truth.

- Three-hundred-sixty-degree reviews can be dangerous. Don't be the first one to review the boss for the record.

- There is no feeling more relieving than showing up at class when you think you're having a test and spotting a substitute teacher. Remember that when you constantly set unreasonable goals for your team.

- Manage the morale, the messages, and the doughnuts. Everything else will fall into place.

- Never babysit the children of your boss.

- A manager doing too much clerical work is a sign of a bad job or a bad manager.

- There is no need to pay for suggestions. Employees will gladly provide suggestions if they believe someone will listen and act. Who stands to gain more than the employees?

6

The Organization and Change or Raising Cain

There seems to be cynicism in most organizations toward change initiatives and reorganizations. I can understand the cynicism. Most of these efforts raise blood pressures to panic level and cause great disruptions without a lot to show for it. Phrases like "rearranging the deck chairs on the *Titanic*," "rotating bald tires," and "same old horses, same old glue" are a little too commonplace. It doesn't have to be that way.

Change happens when people think it is in their best interest. Change is also what happens when you're not looking. Organizations do change. Bosses do change. Markets do change. Technologies do change. Products do change. You change. This is all good, but most people will claim they don't like change, or as Harry Truman said, "If you want to make people mad, change something on them."

The key to change, in your organization or your life, is to recognize it coming and deal with it when it arrives. If you see consultants roaming around your organization with huge pads of organization charts, the organization is about to change. If your spouse comes home every night at 2 a.m. claiming he or she is working late but smells like free hotel body lotion, your marital situation may be about to change. And the big one: If you're worried about your job, you probably should be. Who knows better than you whether you are contributing and whether you are dispensable?

Every conference theme seems to have a change component with catchy slogans like "Challenge for Change," "Embrace Change," and "Take Charge of Change." While at the conference, we probably get up at the same time we always do, watch the same TV programs, and wear the same shoes we wore in college.

We have all heard the exhortations many times that change is a constant and we need to learn to deal with it. Easier to say than do when all your coworkers lose their jobs and you are supposed to do their jobs too. That's not change; that's extra work. When you see the big changes coming, anticipate how you will deal with them and start making contingency plans. Without those plans, change has too much of a chance of working against you.

✖   Everyone in the organization should have a picture of what the organization looks like, whether it be a series of boxes, a map of the planets, a fleet of ships, a multi-dimensional cube, or the NASA moon shot diagram. If it's the latter, go back and try to simplify.

✖   No big change will happen in the company without a technology component.

✖   Big ideas may be for the big offices, but most employees know that it is the small incremental ideas that make a big difference.

✖   Quick and thorough implementation *is* a strategy.

✖   Focus is more important than strategy.

✖   Flattening the organization doesn't necessarily mean anything changes.

✖   There is never one solution to any organizational problem. Choose the best from among difficult alternatives by using clear criteria.

✖   Assume that no one likes or wants to pay consultants. What consultants should do, however, is get things implemented. That may be worth whatever you pay them.

✗   Too much resistance to a new system or change probably means there's something wrong with it. Employees will usually act in the organization's best interest. Listen to them.

✗   As a group of employees once said, "For every system you create, we'll create an equal and opposite system." If employees don't like systems, those systems are almost impossible to implement.

✗   Organization change will not occur unless employees believe it is in their best interest.

✗   Always go after the 80 percent and don't worry about the remaining 20 percent, which is seldom worth the effort.

✗   If unimplemented corporate strategies were pennies, we'd all be rich.

✗   Strategies always look and sound better when announced. Reality sets in the next day.

✗   Project scopes are always better when narrowly defined.

✗   "To what end?" is always a good question to ask at the beginning of a big project.

✗   Never give up on projects until they are implemented.

✗ Don't confuse details or volume with results. Many times a ten-page proposal is better than a 150-page proposal.

✗ Treat all major organizational initiatives like a product and launch them with all the sensing and customer focus of a product launch.

✗ There are no such things as communications, turnover, or morale problems. They are symptoms of other problems—usually autocratic management. Don't try to fix the symptoms. Fix the problems.

✗ The result of week-long executive retreats should be more than a one-line mission that doesn't apply to the organization.

✗ Data is always a very powerful impetus for making decisions.

✗ Real employee involvement means that at least 10 percent of the workforce is engaged in meaningful activities related to organization change or improved operations.

✗ Incremental change should take weeks or months, not years.

✗ All organizations have a mission and a culture. The question is "Are they the right ones?" You don't need to spend a lot of time creating them, but you might want to change one of them.

✗ Organization change happens faster when choices are limited in number—or eliminated.

✗ If senior management doesn't see a need for change, it won't happen, or the attempts will be so painful that people will leave rather than keep trying.

✗ The salespeople should be the organization's cheerleaders and optimists. If they're not, make some changes.

✗ The purpose of the staff is to make the line's jobs easier.

✗ When employees start counting the number of vice presidents, there are too many.

✗ "They" is almost always corporate staff or senior management.

✗ If you're corporate staff or senior management, "they" is everybody else.

✗ Human breaks are often applied when things get going too fast.

✗ Labeling employees as revenue generators or nonrevenue generators will stigmatize the nons.

- Worry more about implementation than strategy—it's harder to do.
- When you hear, "We'll be making hard decisions," someone will be losing his or her job.
- If the company strategy is referred to as the "credenza ware," no one knows what the strategy is.
- End to end still means start to finish, beginning to end, from factory to customer, from here to eternity. The phrase is best used when discussing a process.
- There is a business to be made in fixing the wheels on shopping carts. Consider that before you embark on a grand corporate plan.
- Growth almost always creates bureaucracy.
- Any effort that simplifies and standardizes processes is good. There are exceptions.
- Talking about tool kits often implies easy fixes or magic. Unless you're a carpenter or plumber, be careful how you describe tool kits.
- Too much reorganizing means too much redoing.
- At all costs, avoid dotted-line or ambiguous reporting relationships.

- Reorganization means someone will lose his or her job. Get on the task force that will make the recommendations.

- If you're worried about your job, you probably should be.

- If everyone else is telling you to worry about your job, you probably should.

- Remember the parable about the captain of the battleship steaming through the dark night and who proudly insisted that the ship showing the light dead ahead give way … until the "ship" identified itself as a lighthouse. It applies to many organizational situations.

- Those who do the work should have a say in how it's to be organized.

- Whatever initiatives you are communicating, remember to tell your audience three things: what it is and why, how it will affect them, and when they will know more.

- When consulting, the word *thoughtful* should be a part of the approach section. The "search and replace" option should not be an option.

- The lifespan of any organization's design is less than twenty-four months. Stay tuned if you don't like what you see.

✖ There are very few "standard operating procedures." Those that do exist will soon be changed or eliminated.

✖ In projects and meetings, prepare rigorous lists of things to do with dates—learn to use tools like Gantt charts.

✖ Public compliance with private defiance will kill any change initiative.

✖ Believe that change can happen, even after overwhelming evidence says things never seem to get better.

✖ Watch a big reorganization closely. It will broadcast what will be important in the company.

✖ Every change initiative will have an impact on other parts of the organization; know what the impact might be.

✖ Work elimination should accompany job elimination; someone needs to pay attention to the balance—i.e., with job elimination, work elimination should also occur.

✖ The fastest way to create organizational change is to change people.

- The hard part of any process is determining who decides who decides.

- If the "answer" to an organizational issue is already declared or known, test the answer before you waste time coming up with a new one.

- Real change in any organization usually happens due to an outside impetus.

- Employees always know what's going on in a company. When making announcements, assume no one will be surprised.

- Let the business shape the organization, not the organization shape the business.

- Reducing costs, increasing compensation, or providing more training are usually not the solutions to organizational problems.

- The fewer the policies and procedures, the better.

- Don't confuse the organization chart with who does what. Real activity often takes place between the organization chart lines.

- Organization change initiatives always provide the opportunity to go after cost. Organization change initiatives are often cost-reduction drives in disguise.

- The creation of any organization is a series of compromises.

- Whenever everyone agrees that something is a bad idea, it probably is—so don't try to implement it.

- Most big problems look bigger than they are.

- Real change and success will happen when you hear: "I like it"; "I'll use it on the job"; "I see a change because of it"; and "There's a dollar return in it."

- Anyone whose job title includes the phrase "decision support" probably slows decisions down.

- "Centrally located" means far away for everyone, not just a few.

- Certain parts of our bodies and organizations never die—they have to be killed. Teeth and morale are good examples.

- Working in self-directed teams means there is no traditional foreman or supervisor. Don't let anyone act that way on your team.

- The fastest way to turn the aircraft carrier in the proverbial lagoon is to blow it up and reassemble it facing in the right direction.

- When told you don't understand the big picture, ask to see that big picture.

- Organizations are often like the emperor with no clothes. Everyone talks about how fine the suit is, but the subjects of the kingdom know there is nothing there.

- New company names, logos, and organization charts rarely create change. Change happens when work is altered.

- If your company has had more than two presidents in a year (and everyone says it's just a coincidence), start asking lots of questions.

- There are plenty of other ways to cut costs besides cutting pay.

- Structure is necessary, but bureaucracy is not. Don't confuse them.

- Don't spend a lot of time "witch hunting." In the end, it doesn't matter who did it. Who fixes it matters.

✖   No standards + no measures + no penalties = no direction.

✖   Tweaking organizations will create a lot of tweaks but no real change.

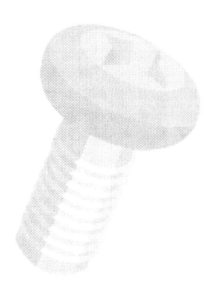

7

Our Menu Has Changed

Like real estate and *American Idol*, customer service (or the lack thereof) is a common discussion piece these days. We want to talk to a real person in customer service, but we don't want to pay for anything extra. We don't want to talk to anyone who is working for an outsourcing firm, but we can't tell the difference. We want to be nice to the customer service person until we know we won't get our way. We want never to be placed on hold. We want always to be correct, and we want them always to be wrong and fix whatever problem they have inflicted upon us. Fast.

On the other side of the equation, customer service reps are sitting in a very large sea of cubes with headsets on. They are dealing with software packages that change on them all the time, supervisors who are putting in new measurement goals, and the woman next to them who is on eBay all day when she is supposed to be answering the phone. At lunch, the same customer service rep needs to run four errands and check on the infant at day care.

It's a situation where everyone is doing their best, but it is still awfully hard.

Airline ticket agents and gate agents are the real warriors of customer service representatives. It's one thing to be sitting in an air-conditioned cube thousands of miles away from anywhere and talking to customers on the phone. It's another thing to be staring across the counter at someone who wants to kill you because a flight was cancelled, which means he or she will miss the most important meeting of his or her life. A true customer service rep takes a beating for something over which they have no control and can't change live in front of the customer.

We are all pleasantly surprised when we make a call and something is resolved: when the airline flight is changed with no extra charge; when the refund is given quickly with no questions asked. Joy, rapture, closure.

It's the closure that matters most. Closure means the rep can close out the account and the customer can go away, happy we hope. Next time you are dealing with customers or service reps, make sure you know that it is closure you seek and rejoice when it comes your way.

✕ Never complain about clients or customers unless you are 100 percent sure it will never get back to them.

✕ You can never be 100 percent sure that complaints will not get back to clients or customers.

✕ Habitual whining about clients or customers will put your career in jeopardy and make you hate your job.

✕ The phrases "Can I put you on hold?" and "Customer Service Department" should never be associated with each other.

✕ When the sign in the customer service department says "Take a number," it is a sign more about the customer service than the process.

✕ Being asked to hold is not a question. It's a message about customer service.

✕ The closer people are to working with a customer, the more willing they are to change.

✕ A casual "We can do that" often means the scope just changed, and it will show up on the next bill.

✕ Make decisions based on what's best for the customer, not on internal rankings.

✕ Benefits are almost always more important than features.

✴   Cutting prices to get business rarely works—and often backfires.

✴   Customer-service-improvement initiatives should receive more attention than others.

✴   Don't sponsor expensive golf tournaments for customers at the same time you're raising prices.

✴   When someone says, "This job wouldn't be bad if it weren't for the people and the telephone," don't put him or her in customer service.

✴   If you ever think, "No matter what we do, they'll come back," think again.

✴   Making people wait for longer than five minutes is rude. Doing it chronically will label you as either rude or a poor time manager. Neither is good.

✴   Giving customers features they are unwilling to pay for means you will either have an overly expensive product or dissatisfied customers.

✴   The customer is not always right. But it's still a good place to start.

✴   Using the F word with a customer service rep will never get you what you want.

- When customer service is the last to know about new products or changes, expect the customers to be similarly uninformed.

- Living in the same time zone as the customer, real or imagined, is greatly appreciated.

- Field service people are the heroes of most organizations.

- When a customer starts preaching about partnering, get ready for a request for a price reduction.

- Be careful when someone in the purchasing department starts saying, "It's a two-way street."

- Be known as someone who enhances customer service.

- Don't be internally focused. Learn what's important to customers and clients.

- Companies like UPS may not do everything right, but they sure keep their trucks clean and their people courteous. There is a lesson in paying attention to details like people and trucks.

- FAQ (Frequently Asked Questions) are not to be ignored. They usually show trends about what's important. If they keep getting asked, it means they are not getting answered.

✘ If you receive a customer complaint letter, give him or her what he or she wants.

✘ If you write a customer complaint letter, tell the company what you want.

✘ Remember what Stanley Marcus said: "You achieve customer satisfaction when you sell merchandise that doesn't come back to a customer who does."

✘ Be wary of slogans like "The Future Is Here" or "Excellence Through People." Look for the beef.

✘ Procurement decisions should be based on what the people who will be using the item(s) need—not just on the cost.

✘ True service means never having to say you're sorry.

✘ Automated customer service is often an oxymoron. Make a change if it is.

✘ When you set up a Helpline or Help Desk, you create expectations. Make sure you can live up to them.

✘ Know where you are in the "value chain" and make sure you're providing value.

- In all sales situations seek clarity—is it sold or isn't it?

- The true test of whether you (and your company) are customer-driven is how you set priorities. If the question "How will this affect customers?" is always the first one asked, the chances are good the organization is customer-driven.

- If you work with a subcontractor, agree on a budget prior to commencing work. At work or on that kitchen remodel.

- Never surprise anyone with the size of your invoice.

- Whenever the scope of a project changes, rates and fees will change also.

- Dogs that beg are annoying. Don't imitate them.

- Never put anyone on hold for longer than one minute, unless the caller enjoys being left on hold.

- *Close to customers* is a relative term. If you can't see them or can't talk to them, you're not close.

- Every call from a customer is an opportunity for a relationship or a screwup.

- If you want to hear the voice of the customer, try answering the phone.

✗   Answering the phone can be a competitive advantage.

✗   Act like the customer is king, even if no one else in your organization does.

✗   Customers don't care how you're organized—they care most about responsiveness, cost, and speed.

Can You Work Like This Dog?

Unless you're a rock star or a professional athlete with an agent behind you, the most important thing to realize when planning your career is: You own it. Owning your career will make it a source of constant ambiguous victories.

Everyone will give you advice, but you must sift out what applies to you from what doesn't. Only you know if you're miserable—despite being in a job everyone envies. Only you know if you're underpaid for your contribution and should be looking elsewhere. Only you know what training you need to be successful. Only you know when you've had enough of your butthead boss and should say, "See ya later."

Some of the variables to consider when evaluating a career are love, money, geography, lifestyle, hobbies, values, and travel. Owning your career means matching these variables with job opportunities, being truly honest with yourself about what you want, and making a decision. That's all. Don't over-engineer your career. Just own it.

There is never time to experiment with your career. But when we're most free to experiment, we tend to play it the safest. I took an informal poll and asked friends and colleagues what career advice they'd give for career changes. The universal answer? Take risks. This advice is especially germane in the current job market. If things don't work out, what do you have to lose? Taking these risks can work to your advantage:

> *Try to contribute quickly.* Given the desire of all organizations to survive and transform themselves, why wouldn't your efforts be welcome?
>
> *Accept a travel assignment.* View it as an adventure. Six months in South America? No problem.
>
> *Guess at what you want to do if you aren't sure.* Not knowing is normal. The risk of trying something you may not like is better than the risk of being idle.

Trust in your own judgment. If your job description is long and detailed, you should work for the government. Otherwise, it should say to do the most important things every day and use your best judgment.

When I think about my past mistakes and what I've learned, I realize that thousands of people influenced who and where I am. Learn from those who have gone before you. The Internet, virtual offices, short hair, and goatees aside, success is still related to passion for your work, learning from mentors, making decisions, owning your career, and taking risks.

- ⚒ Availability is not a skill. Don't think because you are available you will get chosen for the promotion or task force. Some things have not changed since choosing up sides on the playground. If you are not getting chosen, get the skill that will get you chosen. Avoid one of the greatest nebulous defeats at work—never getting chosen for the cool projects or the promotions—by working on skills, not availability.

- ⚒ Those who say, "Do what you love and the money will follow," must love electrical engineering or financial analysis. I doubt that this comes from the people who love fishing or crocheting.

- ⚒ Make sure you get proper credit for previous work experience before you start any new job. It shows up in your pay right away, and if you don't, you may never get the credit. Negotiate between the time the offer is made and your acceptance of the offer. Once you start, the negotiations are over.

- An organization with a reputation that it eats its young and shoots its old is not one to work for unless you are exactly forty.

- In describing your job, if the typical response is, "Nice work if you can get it," keep your job. If the response is, "You're riding on a gravy train with biscuit wheels," work harder to keep it.

- Draw a line in the sand on certain career moves. The line could be relocating, traveling, or …

- It is rare that you take too many risks. Take more.

- The decision criteria for careers can change, but always know what sacrifices you and your family are willing to make.

- Repeatedly saying "someday," "sometime," and "one of these days" is a sign it may be time for a career change. If you catch yourself saying, "I'm trapped," it is definitely time.

- Your skills should look like the letter T. Know a little about a lot of things and a lot about your one thing. Be proud of the one thing for which you are known—it is your brand.

- There are no jobs, only career choices. On second thought, you can turn your career into a job by eliminating all the reasons why you chose your career.

- At work, aim to have your picture on the Wheaties box, not the milk carton. Be known for your accomplishments, not your absence.

- If all that is said is, "... to pursue other interests," everyone will ask what really happened.

- Choose to allow others to make choices about their lives and careers. It will develop their ability to respond. This is doubly true for career choices.

- Counting down the months until retirement should not start before twelve. A long countdown is like the inmate making *###* marks on the wall.

- Most of us are addicted to activity and feel bad if we are not busy. Choose activities that you want to do; don't fill the time.

- Consider all jobs as immersion programs. Being a lifeguard could be an immersion program in oceanography and first aid. Being an executive assistant could be an immersion program in project management and diplomacy.

- If your father or mother runs the company, be the first one in and the last one to leave every day. The standards are always higher when your dad or mom is the boss. Consider that before you take the job.

- In putting, as in life, always err long. If the ball has no chance of reaching the hole, it will never go in.

- Don't choose a job based on its having the latest start date. Or the earliest one.

- Career questions that include the word *still* cast a tentative at best, negative at worst, shadow, as in "Are you still in construction?" No one hears the question "Are you still a brain surgeon?"

- Be known for something of your very own. As San Francisco is to the Golden Gate Bridge, you are to …

- Be free and expansive with career advice for coworkers' children. Someday your own children will be looking for good advice. Find victory by being generous with your time in a world where people are too busy or apathetic.

- When you change jobs and everyone tells you that they are writing your new number in pencil, think again.

- Don't refer to people's work in leadership development, executive education, or training as "soft."

- The Web itself will not offer you a job, but it allows for incredible data gathering.

- Rocky, Bullwinkle, Boris, and Natasha are still a source of career and organizational lessons. So are Attila the Hun, Buddha, Thomas Jefferson, and any person of note that you choose.

- Falsifying your resume on the Web is as bad as falsifying your resume on paper—only faster. Either one can get you fired. Your accomplishments are your victory. Recognizing the room you have to grow is a victory. What you have yet to do is not a defeat.

- There's no need to refer potential employers to your personal Web page. No one will look at it.

- Remember that the Web is a source of information about you as much as it is a source to collect data. Look yourself up to see if those college arrest records are still showing up.

- Don't expect to hear back from employers you contact over the Web all the time. If you do, it's a bonus. If it's an automatic response, don't be offended; you are still special.

- Employers really do hire through their Web sites. Learn how to use them.

- Don't quit your job because your friends do. Don't stay with your job because your friends do. If you're worried about losing your job, you probably should be. If your friends tell you they are worried about your losing your job, you really should be.

- First jobs are like first dates. They may last longer than you had expected.

- Continuing in a career that is only okay is like dating someone you don't want to marry.

- Being directionally correct in career decisions is better than sitting around at home.

- A bad job where you are learning something and making money is better than being idle.

- Tell your children to become chiropractors or opticians. With so many people schlepping computers around, fixing backs and eyes are sure to be growth careers.

- Provide names to search consultants when they call. You may be helping those friends who want a change but don't know it yet.

✗ Learning when to say no may help your career more than always saying yes and not meeting expectations.

✗ The process of negation is sometimes the best way to make a decision. Knowing what you don't want will get you what you do want. This is a particularly useful technique with career decisions.

✗ Trust your instincts. There is a reason other people value your experience. You should as well.

✗ Sweeter than getting the job you've always dreamed of is having the freedom to turn it down.

✗ You're never too old to change, learn a new job, start over, or try something new.

✗ Always check job applicants' references, including relatives.

✗ If you get fired, give yourself two days at most to feel sorry for yourself. Focus on your next job, not your last one.

✗ Take jobs that have an inherent brand recognition— either in the title or in the organization.

✗ Spend job-hunting time with people who can hire you.

✘   Job hunting resembles a target. You are the dot in the middle. The people in the first circle are the ones who know you and like you but are the least equipped or able to help you. The outside circles are the people who are friends of friends and connections. That's where the jobs are.

✘   If you don't send out holiday cards, at least once a year send your key contacts an announcement so everyone is current on your address, phone number, and what you're doing.

✘   Don't finish other people's sentences, especially your boss's.

✘   While looking for a job, check your messages more than usual. Every five minutes.

✘   Resume gimmicks rarely work. Don't glue pennies to your resume or design it so that it folds into a cube.

✘   Don't take a temp job for more than three months unless you love it or it may lead into a job with benefits.

✘   The most devastating word for job seekers is *unfortunately.*

✘   When you get the entrepreneurial urge, go visit someone who's started a business—it may cure you, or you may get inspired to take that risk and follow your passion.

✖   When productivity improvements leave you with nothing to do, find something fast that will grow revenue.

✖   Keep your resume updated.

✖   The photos in recruiting brochures never reflect real life on the job.

✖   "Career path" implies a well-worn route. The truth is that you make your own way running around the organizational bushes and brambles.

✖   Turnover is contagious.

✖   "Find a passion and follow it" is all the career advice you'll ever need.

✖   Regardless of your line of work, never ask, "Are we a profession?"

✖   If your expertise coincides with the company mission, Hallelujah.

✖   Bite off more than you can chew and chew it well.

✖   The hiring process always takes longer than both seekers and employers want.

✖   Landing a job is as much a function of timing as it is qualifications.

✗ Your children can probably help you define what you do ... "My dad helps companies work better." (Management consultant.) "My mom helps companies get known." (Public relations.)

✗ The purpose of a resume is only to get an interview. Don't have ulcers over the color of the paper, print size, or margins. Those issues are not that important to the real people who hire you.

✗ Never tell the person who is interviewing you for a job that he or she looks like a golden retriever.

✗ There are never as many staff jobs as there are line jobs. Remember that landing a job is often a function of probability.

✗ Maintain a keen sense of humor when looking for a job. You'll need it.

✗ The sentence "Salary is secondary to challenge, growth, and opportunity" is one of the great lies.

✗ Convert training into experience as soon as possible.

✗ Giving two weeks' notice on your current job to go to something great is like putting that calculus book away for the final time. Closure in life is rare and worth pursuing.

- When requested to attend a meeting at 4:30 on Friday, and to bring your badge and keys with you, don't go.

- Unexplained absences from the office mean everyone assumes you're out interviewing.

- Intolerance of other views will limit your career advancement.

- Business bestseller lists are a reasonable way to determine what senior management is reading. Read them.

- Life in business is made up of ambiguous victories and nebulous defeats—claim them all as victories.

- As Henry Ford II said, "Never complain, never explain." Be courageous in your business perspectives.

- Articles in business magazines that say things like "You should be earning four times your age" make nearly everyone feel bad. Know that you're not the only one who feels those numbers can't be right.

- There is an inverse relationship between romance and money. The more romantic a product, the less likely that you will make money from it. The real money may be in toilet seats and car mufflers, not wine or sailboats.

- Follow your heart and instincts as much as you follow the analysis. Don't choose between the two; combine the two.

- On average, we all only live for about 25,000 days. Take out the calculator, plot where you are, and don't dwell on what you've missed. Just enjoy the rest. Not through work alone, but through everything that is life.

- Dress codes should say one thing: Wear something inoffensive that would be appropriate if a client or customer showed up unannounced.

- Wear cowboy boots with business suits only if you're from Texas, Oklahoma, or New Mexico, or if you own a herd of cattle.

- Job security is an oxymoron.

- The "cycle of performance" for careers is shortening. You're only as good as your last project.

- Always consider pretending to be smart even when you're clueless.

- Unplanned career moves may be the most exciting. Think of those unusual offers as career dancing lessons.

- Standing at the gate like Auntie Em and waving goodbye to Dorothy as she is about to go into Oz is not where you want to be. Be Dorothy, not Auntie Em.

- Whether affirmative-action programs stay, go, or change, making any decision that discriminates will get you fired.

- "Back office" means you could be a target for reduction or outsourcing.

- The statement "It's just a job" is rarely true.

- Always being below the midpoint in your salary grade means you're never going to make a lot of money.

- If the recruitment advertising asks, "Can You Work Like This Dog?" it's either a great place with a sense of humor or a bad place to work.

- Saying "It beats being a housewife" is not going to get you promoted.

- No benefits, no overtime, no holiday pay means you're very dispensable.

- Crying at work will hurt your credibility.

�֎   Hair always looks good on the way to get it cut. Pain always goes away on the way to the doctor. The car always works great on the way to the garage. And the job always seems pretty good on the way to resign. Be sure.

✖   Organizations that use military time are telling you what it's like to work there. (Airlines are the exception.)

✖   When the early response to a job-seeking inquiry is too good, expect the job to be telemarketing, data entry, or direct sales.

✖   Never curse during an interview, even if the interviewer does.

✖   Start every new job with a sense of zeal you would want others to show.

✖   The fastest way to give yourself a raise is to work fewer hours.

✖   Know if you're a "transaction person" or a "process person." Then learn and use the traits of the other type.

✖   Individual contributor is a label to avoid if you want to be promoted. It usually means people think you lack the ability to lead a team or project.

- Internal transfers are usually painful but worth the trouble if you want to do what you want or get away from what you don't want.

- Being part of a growing company does not ensure career growth.

- Lack of a sense of urgency will eventually lead to lack of a job.

- Honestly assess your value to your employer. If you think you are worth more, then you are worth more. You'll get it eventually.

- Use the Internet to look for jobs, but only at home.

- Once you quit or retire, stay away from your old workplace. They don't miss you.

- Subscribe to the pro athlete school of career planning. We're all free agents and should go to the team that we can help and where our own needs will be met.

- Dual career tracks don't move at the same speed.

- Interim is not a good spot to be in.

- A stint in the military can still be the right career choice. Don't miss it.

- Wear nose rings only if you work for MTV, a messenger service, or yourself.

- There are no job hoppers, only opportunists.

- There is not necessarily a relationship between how long someone is employed and his or her qualifications.

- There is a rhythm to work and to each job. Get in the rhythm; it makes the job easier.

- The race at work is not always won by the swift, and there is more to life than increasing its speed.

- Unless you're a surgeon or an airline pilot, always remember that as much as you like or dislike your job, it's still just a job. But it is your job.

- Get into the office early.

- When you hear words like *restructuring*, *de-layering*, and/or *rightsizing*, get your resume together.

- If you interview for another job, inside or outside the company, expect that your boss will find out; be prepared.

- Resignation letters should only be one or two lines. Don't take parting shots and burn bridges.

✻ Develop friends in the executive search-and-placement business.

✻ Buy clothes that will last a long time. Always have one suit for interviewing.

✻ If you even *think* you're vulnerable, you should probably find another job.

✻ Understand the core of the business and bond with it. Don't take a job at Electronic Arts if you hate video games.

✻ Seek rotational assignments, especially if one will put you in a key operational role of close to the seat of power in corporate headquarters.

✻ Read *What Color Is Your Parachute?* every year.

✻ Maintain a three-year rolling career plan.

✻ Strive to be known as a: • Rainmaker • People Developer • Decision Maker.

✻ Always have an answer to the question "What would I do if I lost my job tomorrow?"

✻ Know what your pay grade is—what the salary range is, where you are in the range, and how to get to the next level.

- If you're in a job where someone ever tells you to look busy, look for another job.

- Do your homework before interviews—reading annual reports, which are easy to get, is the minimum.

- If anticipating your first day of work doesn't stir feelings of excitement in your gut, it isn't the right job for you. Don't find out the hard way.

- When interviewing, think about the people with whom you'd be working. Eight hours a day is a long time to spend with people you don't enjoy.

- Have lunch once a month with someone outside the company who someday might hire you.

- Pick your friends carefully. The water cooler set may be accessible, but those who are there all the time will always be there.

- Do something good early in your new job or assignment.

- Never be the last to leave a company going downhill; your personal market value declines each additional day you stay.

- Money now is worth more than money later.

✖   Manage the paradox of being 100 percent committed to what you are doing while keeping an eye open for other opportunities.

✖   If a job sounds too good to be true, it probably is.

✖   Develop a network of friends and advisers that can give you advice on issues you are dealing with. Think of this as your own personal board of directors.

✖   The most successful people in business are also the most interesting.

✖   The person who spends all of his or her time at work is not hardworking; he or she is boring.

✖   Work for a company where pay equals performance.

✖   Try to make your hobbies into a career.

✖   Own your own career.

✖   Always get a title and sufficient money going into a company; promises about future potential are always overstated.

✖   The concept of entitlement is disappearing fast. You have to earn employment and benefits.

✖   A good raise is 10 percent.

✕   The organization most of us grew up with is gone. Corporate chaos is here to stay.

✕   Hanging around in an office lobby will give you a flavor of what it's like to work in the organization.

✕   Career planning is an oxymoron; the most exciting opportunities tend to be unplanned.

✕   Be loyal to your career, your interest, and yourself.

✕   If your job isn't going well, change jobs before you even think about taking your frustrations out on your coworkers, your family, or yourself.

✕   Before you join an organization based on beliefs, make sure you believe the beliefs.

✕   Always be able to answer the question for yourself and those who work around you, "Why do I work here?" Money is only the start.

✕   If the only answer to "Why do I work here?" is "For the money," start putting a transition plan together.

✕   Get involved in the management of not-for-profit organizations. You can get experience there that you can no longer get in large organizations. Set a time limit of how much you want to give; it can be limitless.

- Keep reading basic personal-finance and investment guides.
- When someone describes your company or products as neither low-cost nor differentiated, think about how long you will be working there.
- Never say no to an offer to relocate without at least considering it.
- When a consultant from a search firm calls, take the call. You never know what pleasant surprises may be on the other end.
- Don't make light or fun of your organization's core business. You will offend everyone who shows up to perform that work on any given day.
- Life is not like the movies. People do lose their jobs, get hurt on the job, and have problems dealing with day-to-day stress. Consider yourself lucky when things are going well and enjoy it.
- Although we don't know it at the time, where we elect to go to college is one of the most important decisions we will make in our lives. Remember that when people ask you for advice about college.

✴ Know the history of your organization. The knowledge might give you some clues about your future there.

✴ When you move up, send your own photo and promotion announcement to the local newspaper if the company won't do it.

✴ Discuss your day when you get home (although not too much). It will help others understand your work.

✴ Don't ever sell anything you wouldn't use.

✴ Know the image you want to project when you join an organization. Reversing first or undesirable impressions is almost impossible.

✴ If accused of checking your brains at the door or asked to do the same, retort with a strong and clear rejoinder and look for another job.

✴ If your organization talks about replacing your job function with technology, don't look for another job doing the same thing. Learn the technology.

✴ Once-in-a-lifetime opportunities are never to be missed. If the opportunity interferes with starting a job, take the opportunity and delay the job.

- Job concern is inversely proportional to the level of contribution you know you are making. The less the contribution, the higher the concern.

- Do not collect or post ding letters when looking for a job. It will only make you feel worse. Instead, frame your offer letter.

- When the raise that you receive is not enough, make sure people know your feelings even if there's no chance that the dollars will change. The commotion may help next time.

- A key element in making a good career decision is the concept of worth. Choose a career from which you or someone else will derive some worth.

- Ignore all bad news about the career field you love and have chosen.

- When considering long-range career plans, think in terms of short increments that will lead somewhere.

- Some people do get hired only because they've been so persistent that human resources wants to get rid of them. Persistence does pay.

- Guarantees of security should never be believed.

✗   Even if you are a great performer, if you quit your job and then change your mind and want to go back, don't expect to get rehired or even considered at the same level.

✗   The biggest job worry should be the opportunities you will miss if you don't experiment or try to improve things.

✗   When choosing a major in college, if you don't enjoy the subject or the classes, you won't like the career.

✗   Don't worry if you're making it up as you go along. Most others are too.

✗   Skills acquired along the way don't ever get wasted. No matter what the job or how far afield, you will drag components of your entire career with you to your next jobs.

✗   If you ever saying anything like "I'm a _____ _____ (fill in the blank: old guy, college graduate, laid-off middle manager, retired military officer …) with no future," change your thinking.

✗   If you believe you have no future, you don't.

✗   If you have changed jobs frequently in a short period of time by either getting fired or quitting, there might be more going on than just meeting the futurists' predictions that we will all have eight careers in our lifetime.

- There are quality programs created to induce minorities into certain careers that are more than lip service. Check them all.

- Don't be surprised if job interview questions are like a case study. Expect to hear sentences like "I'm going to describe a situation to you."

- Choose role models carefully and understand the rewards and sacrifices involved in their success.

- Every job change decision is a big one. Don't underestimate.

- Watch the movie *Planes, Trains and Automobiles* before you choose a career in consulting. You will become Steve Martin.

- For better or worse, the great-paying blue-collar jobs are disappearing. Do anything you can to get through college.

- If you tell your boss you have another offer, be prepared to quit.

- Getting paid for not working serves neither you nor the company. Find something worthwhile to get paid for.

✗   There is no relationship between jobs being open and having them internally. There is always a hidden job market.

✗   No amount of pride should get in the way of finding a job to feed your family.

✗   Never settle for a job, but be realistic about the kinds of jobs for which you are qualified.

✗   Life experience is more important than job experience.

✗   If everyone is making jokes like "Last one out, turn out the lights," make sure you're not the last out.

✗   Meaningful work is when you're both committed and engaged.

✗   Never drink alcohol during an interview, even if the interviewer does.

✗   When you're starting a new job, ask the stupid questions while you can.

✗   Luckily all job candidates believe they can solve the organization's problems as they're revealed during the interview process. Otherwise, no one would ever change jobs.

- An internal promotion is one of the most powerful signals the company can send you about your perceived value. If you're continually passed over, that's also a signal.

- A college degree cannot substitute for experience, but it can help you get ready. Make sure you get experience.

- Create combinations of what you want to do and where you want to live. Play with the combinations as the options roll in.

- Wait until you see your coworkers before you buy your entire wardrobe.

- As the interviewer, droning on about yourself will make all candidates look good. But not you.

- Being labeled as a Subject Matter Expert (SME) is almost always a sign that you are the "go-to" person in a particular area. You now have a reputation, so become an SME in something you like to talk about.

- Optimism will get you farther at work than obnoxiousness.

- How to know if you're an SME (Subject Matter Expert):
  - You believe you could solve world hunger if you turned your attention to it instead of the subject in which you are an expert.
  - You believe you understand what someone means on your subject better than he or she does.
  - You think everyone simplifies things too much.
  - You can find an exception to every rule on your subject.
  - You can dream up unimaginable situations.

9

To Dos and Not To Dos: The Unwritten Code

I once called a candidate for a job early in the morning. Well, not that early to most of the world. It was 9:00 a.m., and he was in college and looking for that great entry-level job. The phone rang in his room, and he answered it by saying, "This better be good." Someone should have told him that when you are looking for a job there are good and bad ways to answer the phone.

There are just some things you do and some things you don't. These are the rules and commonsense ideas that no one may tell you and are not written down, but if you violate them, you are dinged. The candidate previously mentioned did not get that job.

This is a huge category of information I call "the code of too simple not to know." Call it folklore, call it common sense, call it courtesy, call it using judgment that will help you succeed; just don't call it etiquette. These are the pearls of wisdom that may not have a rationale, may not have a basis in quantitative reasoning, but are important.

For some of them I wonder why reminders are necessary. For example, why do I have to remind senior executives to wear clothes that fit? Why do people walk around with toothpicks in their mouths? Why do otherwise normal people use their middle finger as a driving tool?

The code includes addressing any activities that can be seen as acting in poor taste. Firing someone through an E-mail message is in poor taste.

The code changes and morphs all the time as life and technology evolve. New parts of the code are emerging dealing with iPods, text messaging, blogs, and hybrid cars. Since there will never be a written code, it is up to you to always know where the code is moving.

We can all create our own list of what goes on the Not To Do list from our experience. And of course, we can't forget the To Dos from Mom, like wear clean underwear and keep your hands to yourself. Pay attention to those as the constant; just add the new ones that no one tells you but are important.

✖   Never tuck your shirt into your underwear.

✖   Never write a phone number down without putting a name next to it. It's easier than calling all those numbers to see what name matches the number.

✖   Know the difference between wine categories. "Red" and "white" are not enough.

✖   Never make quotation marks in the air with your fingers.

✖   Don't put your company's name on a vanity license plate. You'll have to re-register the car if you get laid off.

✖   In your written work, say something meaningful in the first sentence.

✖   Distill each paragraph into one sentence. Include that sentence in the paragraph.

✖   Start with a rough draft as soon as possible and fill in the details as you go. You'll find the end product will be similar to the original intention.

✖   Use editors and critics. As defensive as we all get, they do help.

✖   Never let anyone you work with see you naked.

- Behavior that you wouldn't want your mom, brother, or sister subjected to is probably harassment. No need for big legal manuals, use that as your guide.

- Learn what a collar stay is and use it.

- Use your clients' products. Don't give a presentation to Apple on a Dell PC or rent a Ford to call on Chrysler or General Motors.

- Worry more about doing the right thing than being politically adept.

- Have a professionally done black and white photo of yourself always ready for publicity and other uses. Never allow yourself to be put next to the wall for a photo.

- When people you respect recommend books, read them.

- The harder it is to write a brochure about your organization, the less clear what the organization is all about.

- Give money to your alma mater(s), no matter how little the amount.

- Go to trade shows but be realistic about their benefits, which are to stay up to date on products and competitors and to network. Learn who has the best parties and who is giving out the best souvenirs.

- Use New Year's resolutions as a real way of setting goals.

- Casey Stengel said that some people make things happen, some people watch things happen, and some people say what happened. Be in the first category.

- Don't be afraid to collect bills.

- Pay your bills, or at least let your vendors know when they will be paid. Make sure their expectations are always met.

- Learn what the labor movement is all about, how it's changing, and what it means to your industry. Be unbiased as you learn.

- Spend time understanding what "real work" is, like working on an assembly line, picking grapes, or driving trucks. It will ground you in reality.

- Learn what "vesting" means, how it applies to you, and when it will kick in.

- Don't use overhead projectors.

- Never have more than three people from your side in a sales call.

- Develop intense curiosity and gather information about topics such as retirement and saving for college educations.

- If you call the Help Line or Help Desk, be nice to the people who answer the phone. It's an impossible job.

- Don't be mean to service people, especially restaurant or hotel help; it only embarrasses those around you—and rarely changes anything.

- Write things down in your calendar—even if you're sure you'll remember.

- Learn the difference between harassment and a very demanding boss.

- Point your skis down the hill at work and just go. Going sideways and backwards is a much more painful way to get down the same hill.

- Ignore National Bosses Day.

- Go to your high school reunion. It's a good time to reflect on whether or not you turned out as planned.

- Damned if you do and damned if you don't are never quite equal. Pick the one that you believe is right.

- If the birds are crashing into your office window, put a decal or something on it to save them from being knocked out or worse.

- Read *Good to Great* for a real business book.

- Know at least one restaurant where you can take a client or associate and not have to worry about people finding you or about the quality of the food.

- Retirement planning can be summed up in two words: Save money.

- Know where the public restrooms are on the routes you usually travel.

- The three most important things to keep track of are: expenses, important phone numbers and addresses, and the last flight home.

- Send fan mail.

- Be known as someone who builds bridges, not fences or bombs.

- Brag about someone to another person; that someone is bound to find out.

✗   Simplify, don't complicate—especially processes, procedures, and policies.

✗   Never take a problem to your boss without some solutions. You are getting paid to think, not to whine.

✗   Know what shoes to wear and keep them in proper shape.

✗   Carry telephone numbers with you—use the back of your calendar or an electronic gadget.

✗   Don't write memos of more than one page, and use graphics where you can.

✗   Never miss deadlines. Ever.

✗   Always have documents proofread. Never send a document with a typo.

✗   Never go into a meeting without your calendar.

✗   Collect business cards and keep them in some form. If you don't think you'll remember how you know the person, make a note on the card. They can be like currency.

✗   If you're in a job that requires paying attention to regulatory compliance issues such as tax, employment benefits, or Sarbanes-Oxley, make sure you pay attention to everything.

- Maintain an accurate mailing list for announcements, newsletters, and sales calls.
- Go to the company holiday party.
- Don't get drunk at the company holiday party.
- Keep track of expenses, or you'll end up losing money. Submit expense reports early and often.
- Always carry your business cards with you and give them out freely.
- Always have an agenda.
- Don't micromanage your people, your projects, or your own life.
- Keep a toothbrush and toothpaste in your desk and use them after lunch.
- Write down ideas—they get lost like good pens.
- The buzzwords come and go, but know what is current.
- Never in your life say, "It's not my job."
- Go only to those training classes that will help you. Avoid those that will be a waste of time. Good training classes will expose you to new and exciting ideas.

- Use a spiral-bound notebook to take meeting notes and record voice-mail messages. It will become your business journal.
- Maintain a sense of adventure—there are many things to do if your travels take you to Cleveland in February.
- Complete surveys and return them.
- Help other people network for jobs—what goes around comes around.
- Recognizing someone else's contribution will repay you doubly.
- Buy good luggage and briefcases—people notice.
- The days of the three-martini lunch are over. Don't drink at lunch unless you don't plan to go back to work.
- Take evening and extension courses.
- Make a "to do" list every day. Crossing things off the list is very satisfying.
- Cooperate with consultants—their input can change your life.

- Try not to date coworkers. If you do, be careful. Never date your boss.

- Don't tell people their ideas are bad unless you've got a better one.

- Make friends with the guard in the lobby; someday you will forget your ID badge.

- Don't talk about your boss, clients, or projects in elevators or taxis.

- Let things go. If the old way doesn't work, don't keep it.

- Never make up an acronym; try not to use them.

- Use commuting time well. Listen to National Public Radio, books on tape, or music you enjoy. If using public transportation, read, do paperwork, or get mentally prepared for the day.

- Cultivate a reputation for being reliable and hardworking, even if it means bucking peer pressure.

- Always plan your day while in the shower.

- Keep your desk clean and you will think better.

✖ Avoid being assigned for longer than a year to the human resources department, unless HR is your passion.

✖ Learn how to involve the right people in your work.

✖ Give informational interviews.

✖ Have your own document retention program; if you haven't referred to a file in twelve months, get rid of it.

✖ Keep the good pens in your desk; otherwise, you lose them.

✖ Create work teams with the best available talent, regardless of function or background.

✖ Don't create layers.

✖ Always have a beginning, middle, and end, whether it be a presentation, a meeting, a memo, or a letter.

✖ Never sacrifice quality to make numbers.

✖ Learn the difference between benchmarking and best practices.

✖ Most problems can be lumped into three types: organizational, process, or cultural. Although they are not unrelated, know which is which. Understanding the category will help you derive solutions.

- Read the fine print in early retirement packages.

- Learn the paradoxes of organization work, like growing the organization while maintaining cost controls.

- Be a supporter of the latest fad, but don't build your career around it.

- Get assigned to a project team working with external consultants. You may learn something and protect your job at the same time.

- Learn the definition of outsourcing and find out whether or not you are a target.

- Eliminate guilt: Don't cheat on expense reports, taxes, benefits, or your colleagues.

- Don't smoke. Especially don't hang around in front of the building with other smokers.

- Follow Stephen Covey's suggestion of knowing how to distinguish what's important and what's urgent.

- Always know the answer to the question "What business are we in?"

- Use the word *paradigm* no more than once a month.

✗   Read your junk mail occasionally. It will tell you who is selling what and where people think there are dollars to be made.

✗   If there is a Phase One, the project could take years. Plan accordingly.

✗   Throw away any ties or scarves with any kind of oil stain on them. The stains never come off, and people notice.

✗   Understand basic statistics so you can tell when someone is using them to lie.

✗   Encourage any channel or forum for good ideas.

✗   If you figure out a way to save time, don't waste that time. See what else you can do that is fun or productive or both.

✗   Paying fees, even high ones, is worth it if those fees provide a big return, even in peace of mind.

✗   Rearrange any meeting room until everyone feels comfortable, even if it means stopping the meeting temporarily.

✗   Learn how to really listen to what people are telling you. If you're trying to tell someone something and you can see that he or she doesn't get it, tell him or her in a different way.

- Don't let people make paper clip chains at your desk.
- Don't spend a lot of time telling people what they already know.
- Make morale on Monday morning the same as it was on Friday afternoon.
- Take diversity training seriously.
- Keep a bag of candy hidden in your desk for emergencies.
- Even though most people don't like National Executive Assistants Day (except florists), we still have to celebrate it.
- Know the fire/earthquake escape route from your office.
- Be aware and vigilantly careful when reciting or punching in credit card numbers. Someone could be watching or listening.
- Never dress up for Halloween as the chairman of the board or a hooker.
- If all the office cleaners know your name, you're working too hard.

- If you're entitled to overtime pay, claim it. If you're gaming the system, don't claim it. Someone will catch on.

- Read *USA Today* for trends, the *New York Times* for depth, and the comic strip *Dilbert* for truth.

- Wordsmithing is never done well in a committee.

- Use your cell phone in the bathroom only if you have to call 911.

10

The Person with the Most Frequent Flyer Miles Is Not the Winner

"Should I stay or should I go? If I stay, there will be trouble. If I go, it will be double." This classic line from The Clash could be the anthem for all road warriors. No activity conjures up as much dread and excitement at the same time as business travel.

Whether the mode is airplane, train, or car, the hassle inherent in travel is a constant challenge to determine how wily and patient we can be. Kurt Vonnegut once wrote, "Peculiar travel suggestions are like dancing lessons from God." He was right.

The rules of travel are changing all the time. With security so tight at airports and other key terminals, the travel gods really have us on our toes. There are some general rules about travel that might help you deal with the dancing lessons.

Know where to set your expectations. Southwest Airlines' contribution to the world of travel and business is that they taught us how to set expectations. Whenever I travel on Southwest, my expectations are met because they are so low. I expect to take off and land in a little airport, with no food, no reserved seat, and no first class. They meet these expectations every time. When I travel on most major airlines, I expect much more, but I rarely get it. The conclusion is that if you always set your expectations low, they will almost always be met, and it will help your blood pressure.

Don't be cheap. I once flew across the US with my two sons, one infant and one two-year-old. The infant sat on my lap since I didn't want to buy him a ticket, and the two-year-old sat next to me in the window seat. I was in the middle seat with a very large person whom I did not know sitting on the aisle. By the end of the flight, I was ready to tell the enemy anything they wanted. In fact, as a result of that flight, I still have a severe case of claustrophobia.

Bring more entertainment than you think you will need. The chances that there will not be a good radio station or that the movie won't play are reasonably high. You can only read the LAVATORY OCCUPIED sign for so long until you have to switch to the deep meaning of LIFE VEST UNDER SEAT.

Know and accept the counter-intuitive nature of travel and never try to understand it. There is a snowstorm in Rochester and all the flights between Memphis and Dallas are canceled. People order Bloody Mary mix in abundance in the air when they would never drink it on the ground.

It costs more to fly from Portland to Seattle than it does to fly from San Francisco to Paris. The deeper mysteries of the universe will be solved before some of these.

The difference between having a successful trip or not is embedded in these general rules. A never-ending string of ambiguous victories is yours if you follow them. There are some pluses to travel; it is one of the few times that there is quiet, and it can provide time to reflect and plan. Travel time is also the time to catch up on your reading.

Another big plus is that travel gets you "out there." The adventure that is travel means you never know whom you will meet or what you will learn and you get to experience the possibilities in the unknown. If you stay at home all the time, you pretty much know the possibilities.

The price is the stress and the wear and tear on the body.

After a continuous diet of travel one year, my wife announced that I had morphed from being boyishly good looking to ruggedly handsome to weather-beaten. It made me stop and reflect on the dancing instructions I was getting from God.

⚒ If the sound of the zipper on your luggage makes your children cry, you're traveling too much. If the flight attendants know your name, you're traveling too much. If the short-term parking lot has a space reserved for you, you're traveling too much. If you wake up every day not knowing where you are, you're traveling too much. Get a life.

- It doesn't happen very often, but when airline employees go above and beyond, write letters to the airlines commending them. It does matter to them when it comes time for pay and promotion.

- Write critical letters about airline employees when warranted. It does show up on their permanent records. Some airlines no longer require their employees to give their names. If you can't get a name, use the flight number and any information you can; the letter will find the right home.

- The most dreaded words for the business traveler who has memorized the 800 number for all airline reservation services are:
  - Unfortunately
  - Good news and bad news
  - Shuttle bus
  - Talking to maintenance
  - Reservation was not guaranteed
  - Do you have a confirmation number?
  - Trying a new menu …
  - That bag has to be checked
  - The president is in town
  - We've been notified by Air Traffic Control …

- If the airline gate agent calls you to the counter, something either very good or very bad is about to happen to you.

✖   Compiling the most frequent flyer miles does not make you the winner. It makes you someone who has chosen a career with travel that will take you to far-flung and exciting places. Being the winner of the frequent flyer contest is always at great expense.

✖   On redeye flights, you're sleeping even when you think you're not. It's not a good sleep, full of tossing and crazy thoughts, but you're there faster than you expected.

✖   On an airplane, when the person in front of you slams his or her seat back, the angle makes it impossible to view your computer screen. Put your tray up and put your computer on your lap—thus the name "laptop."

✖   Don't make airline delay stories as long as the delay.

✖   There should be a timer in each airplane lavatory that limits how long anyone can be in there.

✖   You're on too many airplanes if you can't sleep without a seatbelt on or, while in bed, you try to put a seatbelt around your blanket so the flight attendants can see it.

✖   Expect hotel hookups to your computer to be inoperable. Never expect to find an outlet in an airport that will allow you to recharge your computer batteries.

�✗ Airport parking is stressful enough; make sure you know height limits before you get in line to park your SUV with the big roof rack on top.

✗ The skill of smashing bags of ice without breaking the plastic is best learned from flight attendants. Other key skills to learn are: how to eat while standing up, how to knock on the window, and how to signal for emergency exits.

✗ A photo of a newscaster on the back of taxi receipts does not make false expense reports more believable.

✗ It's good that the reliability is better on space shuttles than on moving sidewalks and escalators in airports.

✗ Never underestimate the bad breath that airplane food can induce.

✗ Give up on trying to work on your computer and eat an airplane meal at the same time.

✗ Clean clothes are lighter than dirty clothes; although dirty ones are easier to pack. Always start a trip with clean ones. On the road, sometimes it's easier to buy new clothes than it is to try to get dirty ones cleaned.

✗ Stealing stuff from hotels makes your luggage heavier and hotels more expensive.

✖   Sometimes the most productive work is done when stuck in an airport near a phone and an electrical outlet.

✖   When traveling, don't call home and expect to speak to your children during their favorite TV show, especially if it's *The Simpsons*.

✖   If you take your family with you on a business trip, expect to be ill prepared.

✖   Airplane cart management is when you time your visits to the bathroom so that you don't interfere with the food or beverage cart.

✖   Airport security could be the subject of an entire book. The stories are legion. A random search of the passenger in front of me, a seven-year-old cutie, generated a pencil sharpener to go with her colored pencils for a long trip. The sharpener was confiscated, and the tears ensued. The moral?

✖   Airport security is frustrating and makes you want to tell sarcastic jokes. Never joke around airport security.

✖   First-class flights mean never having to check an appropriate-sized carry-on bag.

✖   Anytime you go back to your hotel room, expect the maid to be cleaning it.

�֎   If you're going to watch the movie on an airplane, rent the headphones.

�֎   If you can avoid it, don't fly with your boss or your client. You don't want them to see you sleeping with your mouth hanging open.

✖   The long lines; the quality of the help; the random, humiliating searches; and the tension of missing your flight are now part of the travel process. There is no predicting which security line will move fastest.

✖   Be prepared to lose anything that you put in the seat pocket in front of you.

✖   Expect that anything you lose on an airplane you will never see again.

✖   Never wear a workout suit or sweat clothes when flying.

✖   No need to start a collection of mending kits and shoe mitts even though hotels are giving them away. No matter the child's age, they won't count as a gift.

✖   If you think the plane is going to crash, keep your shoes on.

✖   Too much travel will make you crazy and unhealthy.

✖   There are two ways to travel: first class and with children.

- Once in a while, sit in a window seat and look out the window to renew your sense of wonder at how airplanes even leave the ground.

- Someday you will have to fly with children. Be gentle to those who are sitting next to you screaming while they color in Barney coloring books.

- Reward yourself and truly savor success by upgrading on return flights.

- Two of the most dreaded words in the English language are *shuttle bus*. If you know the shuttle is part of the routine, see if there is an alternative.

- Don't fight with hotel service people. Relax, let them do their work, and tip them appropriately.

- When traveling, don't get in the habit of buying gifts everywhere you go. If you are somewhere and see a great gift, get it.

- Talk to people on planes. (I keep changing my mind on this one.)

- If you can help it, don't fly on weekends for business.

- Always allow more time than you think to get to the airport. Especially in New York City.

- Flying standby equals middle seat divided by length of flight times time to wait for next available first-class seat.

- Applying fingernail polish while on an airplane is like flossing your teeth on an airplane. Some things should be done in private.

- There's nothing to do about airplane delays. Don't get upset—use the time productively.

- The "eyes glazed over with frustration" look works nearly as well as yelling and is better on the blood pressure.

- Kill time on the "where you need to be" end, not the "where you're leaving from" end. The variables are easier to control.

- Wait until they call your row before you stand at the door leading to the airplane.

- We all like to sit in seats that recline; we just don't like to sit behind seats that recline. Think of that when you push the button and slam back.

- Airplane-crash jokes are not funny.

- Airline headphones will only be comfortable for a short time. Save them for the movie.

✴   Sit in your own assigned seat on an airplane until the door is closed.

✴   Tuck your tie into your shirt when eating on airplanes.

✴   Use airplane time to reflect and set goals. It may be the closest thing to quiet time you ever get.

✴   The quality of a hotel can be determined by its coat hangers. The harder they are to use, the cheaper the hotel.

✴   Leave 90 percent of material you collect at trade shows in the hotel. Take the tchotchkes and goodies home for the kids.

✴   Don't check your luggage, and take only the essentials with you. Travel light.

✴   Always keep your passport and airline tickets in the same pocket of your suit or briefcase.

✴   Never tell someone on an airplane to keep his or her baby quiet.

✴   Expect to get in a fistfight with anyone you tell to keep his or her baby quiet.

✴   At most, only half the time you spend on a plane will be productive; plan accordingly.

✖   Befriend your travel agent, and don't be afraid to demand service.

✖   Be realistic about how much work you can accomplish at night or on a trip and only pack that much. Don't over-pack your briefcase and lug too much around.

✖   There is no relationship between crowding the door to the jet way and getting your pre-assigned seat.

✖   Call home every night when you're on the road.

✖   Never travel in first class if your customer and your boss don't, even if you've used a cheap upgrade coupon.

✖   Don't try to save money on travel expenses if it means you'll lose a productive minute working on whatever you are traveling for.

✖   The little hole that your bag has to go through on the security-check conveyor belt is rigid. If it doesn't fit, it doesn't fit.

✖   Never complain about jet lag.

✖   Never complain about the de-icing process during a blizzard.

- Arguing with security personnel at checkpoints is like arguing with an umpire, only worse. The security people will have you arrested.

- When traveling internationally, read a simple travel guide in advance and carry a quick reference guide to currency exchange.

- Always carry a paperback with you when traveling. Never get on an airplane without something to read. If the person next to you has nothing to read, give him or her something to read.

- Expect your laptop batteries will never last as long as the flight, regardless of the duration.

- Don't be away from home for more than three days at a time—if you can help it.

- Find out if anyone from work is staying in the hotel room next to you before you do anything you wouldn't want them to hear.

- If, while in your underwear, you lock yourself out of your hotel room, call the front desk and hide beside the ice machine.

- Don't charge hotel movies to clients. Never put it on expense reports.

✴   Rejoice if you don't have to take a shuttle bus to get to your rental car.

✴   When traveling with your boss, make sure you have good directions. If you get lost, you'll get blamed.

✴   Even if you travel more than they do, don't share your travel war stories with flight attendants.

✴   Look behind you before you slam your airline seat into a reclined position. If there's a lap baby or anyone using a computer, keep your seat in the upright position.

✴   The flush button in airplane lavatories is always hidden. To make it more interesting, the flight attendant call button and the flush button look similar and are always close to each other. Pushing the proper button is yet another way for the frequent traveler to triumph over confusion and snicker at the less lavatory astute.

✴   When going on a business trip, pack the night before and remember that the x-ray machines will show what you have packed.

✴   Avoid taking golf clubs on business trips unless the trip is specifically intended for golf.

✴   Never take carry-on luggage that's bigger than your car.

- Children are always interested in reading the laminated safety card in the seat pocket. Encourage it.

- Assume that you will not be able to find the light switches or thermostats in hotel rooms. Until there is some standardization, which there will never be, assume you will enter stumbling around in the dark in a room that is too hot or too cold.

- Never trust a hotel clock-radio alarm. Never believe you will be able to figure out how a hotel clock-radio works.

- Checking voice mail from the road more frequently than once every fifteen minutes is a sickness.

- Life in business is more and more like dog years: One year of business life equals seven years of regular life. If you travel a lot, there is a multiplier effect and the equation is worse.

- If you think you'll need a rental car, you probably will. Taxis are only an efficient travel mode in big cities. The bigger the city, the more efficient.

- Develop your own system for airport security lines:
    - Know which line to move to based on who is in line in front of you.
    - Wear shoes that are easy to get off and on.

- If traveling with your boss, when you take your shoes off, know your boss will look at your feet.
- Dump the rodeo belt buckles and jewelry long before you get to the airport.
- Watch which airport security people are most efficient and go to that line. Friendliness is not a variable to consider.

11

Geeks, Grinds, and Gadgets

The other day on the elevator I heard a guy boasting that while he was in a two-hour meeting he had received sixty voice mails. Although I thought about having a contest with him about who had more messages, I stopped and thought, "Are we crazy?" It was like the time I got in a contest about who had the most frequent flyer miles. I don't want to win either of these contests.

That same day I received a call from our systems administrator, never good news. He told me I needed to erase E-mails because I was slowing down the system. I said, "How could that be? I only open the messages in which I have an interest."

He said, "That's the problem; you have 2,000 unread messages." Always the competitor, I asked if that was a record, knowing that my passwords would be changed as a result of my impertinent question. It was nowhere near a record, but, hey, it wasn't I who sent all those unwanted messages to me.

Those two incidents made me reflect on good tools gone bad. Voice mail and E-mail are two of the greatest efficiency tools ever invented, but they are being abused and often make us less effective, not more. No wonder so many executives cite airplane time as the time for reflection.

New tools continue to emerge, but I'm not sure they are helping us as we had hoped. In fact, I think a lot of great tools have become instruments to make our life harder.

It's not a new phenomenon. Paper clips were probably the first efficiency tool that was loved, until they were used to attach pink slips to paychecks. Those little black alligator clips were another real breakthrough and took a load off those broken and bent paper clips. I once had a bunch of Russian cosmonauts as my guests who were fascinated by those clips as a great invention. Now the clips are best known for holding PowerPoint presentations together, the content of which could easily be handled by a paper clip.

Yellow stickies changed the paradigm until they started to appear on everyone's computer at night with messages like "See me ASAP" or "Do these twenty pages over again."

Another tool that I worry is going bad at an accelerating pace is the conference call. It is a great communications tool that can keep people close to home and reduce time wasted.

But conference calls are starting to have a volume problem too. No, not that they are too loud, but that there are way too many.

On a recent rainy day, my calendar listed six hours of back-to-back conference calls, so I worked from home. I needed to participate in the calls, but I was desperate to review a proposal that needed my completion. My seven-year-old son, home from school sick that day and rooting around for something to do, agreed to listen to a few hours of the calls in exchange for turbo allowance. We put the calls on the speakerphone, which allowed him to play nearby while he listened for my name. Whenever he heard my name, he got me and I jumped on the call.

We created time to be together, and I could multitask and get *all* that needed to be done, done. Had my son been pulling at my sleeve for attention while I felt miserable about the proposal that was not getting done, it would have been a disaster of a day.

There is always a delicate balance between the task and the time you allot for it.

Tools can help if you create a balanced arsenal of tools and use them as appropriate. The most effective tool is still talking and listening. The others are surrogates. When you can, you should still be human and treat others the same way. Using efficiency and ease of use as criteria, the following is my view of great and not-so-great innovations.

Greatest Business Innovations of the Last Fifty Years

Yellow stickies	To the office what duct tape is to the home.
Wheelies	A back-saving device that turned almost all baggage rectangular.
Tetris/Solitaire	A justification to carry around a $10,000 PC.
Etch-a-Sketch	The training tool for reading any PDA.
Scan button on the car radio	Allows you to multi-listen while speaking on the phone.
Virtuality	Allows you to be anywhere and work—or not.
Self-adhesive postage stamps	Why did it take so long?
Cigarette lighter in cars	Created the hole to plug in car phones.
Felt-tip pens	The ultimate doodle machine.
Conference calls	What other tool allows us to attend meetings without being there?

Worst Business Innovations of the Last Fifty Years

Powdered cream	A cup of coffee ruined.
The cubicle	Is it a space or not? Is it yours or not?
Resume-scanning software	How does it test for "fun to work with"?
Passwords	Some require four characters, some six, some eight, some a capital letter—all of which make them hard to remember.
Break-out groups	The outcome of the group effort is almost always large sheets of paper never to be used.
Shuttle buses	Add a degree of difficulty to everything.
The seat pocket in front of you	A euphemism for a lost-items container or garbage collector.

✷ Carry an extra computer battery with you no matter where you are going.

✷ Computer icons don't necessarily mean what you think they do. Double-check before you double-click.

✷ Think of the plastic packaging on CD covers and toothbrushes when designing your security system.

✷ Your mother's maiden name is more important than she ever thought considering how many people in security ask for it.

✷ Expect that every message you send or receive is being monitored.

✷ "Unable to find path to server" should not be the command that means take the rest of the day off.

✷ Write down computer passwords somewhere. Probably not on your computer.

✷ Tech Support taking your computer away for upgrades with promises that you will never notice the changes is like the dentist saying there will be some discomfort.

✷ Killer apps are a rare and wonderful thing. They are not a part of anyone's anatomy.

✗ Early adopters and early adapters are not the same.

✗ Employee online chat rooms and message boards are a good source of information and gossip about any organization. Recognize that it is the bucket for every complaint and not a repository for the positive.

✗ Even if it requires an engineer, fix your office chair so that it is comfortable.

✗ Web sites are almost always secure. Who is looking over your shoulder at the computer screen may not be.

✗ "Message erased" is as good as "checked that one off."

✗ Never buy a toy, piece of software, or computer game that features "piercing electronic noises" on the box.

✗ Don't ask a computer system to do what you wouldn't ask the organization to do.

✗ Put at least one game on your computer to get warmed up.

✗ Never get caught with a game on your screen.

✗ Technology eventually evens out. Compete on service and talented people.

- Don't use obscene screen savers.

- Organizations monitor who's doing what on the Internet. Remember, you're supposed to be working.

- Parts lists are not the same as technical manuals.

- Never put a glazed doughnut on a mouse pad.

- A bad phone system can shut down the entire plant.

- Keep track of how much time you waste between chatting on your cell phone and surfing the Web and think of how that time could be better spent. Writing a book? Solving world hunger? Redesigning the DMV?

- There are more ways to communicate than there is content to communicate. Between phones, voice mail, E-mail, instant messages, and little pink slips that say "While You Were Gone," there can't be that much left to talk about. No longer is the "medium the message"; the message is lost in the medium.

- In our virtual world, never underestimate how important it is to talk to one another. Not because we have to but because we need to.

- Never underestimate the tracking potential that can be put to use to learn what you've been doing on the Internet.

- When working on the computer, save the document you're working on frequently. Very frequently.

- Make sure you can operate or fix the printer, fax machine, photocopy machine, and report-binding machine.

- Be the first to use technology—don't fight it. People talk about the Luddites, but they're history.

- Technology cannot solve all problems. It only can make the real work cheaper, faster, and less tedious.

- Technology makes geography no big deal.

- The words *computer conversion* are usually a signal that work will be done manually for a while.

- PowerPoint is not a solution; it's a presentation format. Learn how to use it.

- When nothing is being projected, turn the projector off. The noise, the heat, the distraction—need more reasons?

- The more sophisticated the computer or phone system, the more time people spend figuring out the system rather than doing real work.

- Be known as someone who is able to set a VCR timer and will do so rather than watch 12:00 blink incessantly. Also on that known-for list is: create backup files, make DUDs, and fix a printer.

- Negotiating by using E-mails or fax machines may save you a lot of emotional energy.

- When mysterious things show up on your computer screen, it's never a good sign. Call the help desk, the computer dealer, or the cavalry.

- Learn the basic and current Internet lingo. Never assume others will know it.

- In these days of incredible technological breakthroughs, still be joyous if you can connect from any remote location.

- BlackBerry usage is as addictive as crack cocaine.

- Give your thumbs dancing lessons when you buy your BlackBerry.

Voice Mail

To Review Your Messages, Pound

- If the number of voice-mail messages is overwhelming, take them in batches of five or ten. Avoid skipping the mean and onerous ones; they are probably the ones you need to listen to most.

- Put your own voice on your voice-mail greeting. Make it a professional message with an upbeat tone.

- Know which messages to automatically delete without listening to them. Voice-mail karma smiles on you when you have messages that are easily deleted.

- Remember that voice-mail messages marked *Private* cannot be forwarded, but can be transcribed.

- The first four words of every voice-mail message at work should be, "Hi, _________ (fill in name), __________ (fill in a number) things."

- Assume that if you hesitate at the end of a voice-mail message or say goodbye, anything you add to the message will not be heard.

- In your voice-mail greeting, tell people how to bypass the greeting so that they may leave you a message more quickly if desired.

- Voice mail is like an inbox. Handle each call once and don't let them pile up too high.

- Don't talk faster on voice mail when leaving your number.

- Change your voice mail if you're on vacation, out of town, or need to convey a specific message. It doesn't have to be every day.

- Today 75 percent of business calls go directly into voice mail. Manage voice mail or answer the phone.

- If you give callers only one minute to leave a message, get a new message system. The only one-minute message anyone will leave is "Call me back."

- "Message marked private" can make the heart skip a beat.

- A productive day is not necessarily one in which you have sent a lot of messages.

- Days should not be measured in the number of phone messages received or sent.

- You are more worried about being efficient than effective if your day is measured by voice mails received or returned more than by what you accomplished.

- If the greeting "Welcome to our voice-mail system" makes you cringe, you're behind on your job.

- Beware those who mark all of their voice mail *Private.*

- If you don't want to or can't talk, don't answer the phone.

- Use voice mail as a personal effectiveness tool, not a source of guilt for what you haven't done. Don't skip messages that make you feel like you haven't done something, and especially don't store them. The problem won't go away. Listen to the message, see what needs to be done, delete the message, and take care of the problem.

- Never leave voice-mail messages for someone at night that you'll regret in the morning.

- If voice-mail systems keep cutting you off when you leave messages, your messages are too long.

- If people aren't listening to your voice-mail messages, they are either too long or you're not saying anything.

- Don't let people know you always use the voice-mail delete code before you listen to their messages.

- When people tell you, "You're impossible to reach," they're really telling you:
  - "I need more attention."
  - "You didn't call me back."
  - "You're slowing down decisions."
  - "You're killing yourself; readjust your schedule."

Cell Phones
Are You Still There?

- Always travel with a cell phone. It will save you the time and trouble of the customer service line.

- Don't stand next to phone booths when talking on your cell phone. The reception is no better and it will be quieter somewhere else.

- Borrowing someone's cell phone is okay to find lost friends or to call for pizza deliveries. Otherwise, it is like borrowing someone's toothbrush.

- Learn how to make noises that sound like heavy static in case you need to get off a cell phone.

- "What time is it over there?" is not the question you want to overhear from the person who is borrowing your cell phone.

- Cell phones are for getting work done while in the car; they are not an excuse to keep the kids quiet.

- God invented cell phones for two reasons. The first is so that you can call to say you're running late. The second is for calling the pizza delivery service from the road so that they can be met at your door.

E-MAIL
Server Not Responding

- When responding to an E-mail, double- then triple-check the forward and CC addresses. Jobs have been lost with errant messages being sent to the customers or the boss.

- Expect that every E-mail message you send or receive is being monitored.

- Pay attention to the "Re:" line in E-mail and make it more creative than "Read Me." The "From:" and the "Re:" lines dictate what is read.

- Make sure your E-mail distribution lists are updated so there aren't fifty people getting messages they shouldn't.

- Don't send anything via E-mail that you wouldn't want to appear in your personnel file.

- Using E-mail is a good way to get hard-to-reach people.

- Don't stop doing real work every time your computer beeps with new E-mail.

- E-mail always shows date and time. Use it to your advantage by sending messages before or after regular work hours. It's a good way to show how hard you are working.

- Assume that any attachment to an E-mail message will be neither launched, detached, nor read.

- Sending lewd material out via E-mail will get you fired.

- Using all capitals letters on E-mail is the electronic version of screaming. It's an attention grabber, but it's hard to read and hard to know what's being emphasized.

Conference Calls
Did Someone Just Join?

- Learn how to run an effective conference call. The more dispersed the group, the more important good leadership is. Get help if you need it.

- Always know everyone who is on the other end of any call. Too many side comments and private conversations are lost because of a lack of ear count.

- Never get dressed up for a conference call. Know the difference between a teleconference and a videoconference.

✕   If a global conference call is scheduled for the middle of the night, make sure the participants know what time it is where you are.

✕   Going "global" means you can be on a conference call any time of the day or night.

✕   If there is heavy breathing on a conference call, the host should gently ask that someone to apply nasal strips, wake up, or move the receiver away from his or her face.

✕   On audio conference calls, don't go through overhead slides. Guest speakers can be very informative and effective, but don't let them talk about anything that those on the call can't see.

✕   Stop to get gas before you get on a conference call from your car, not during.

✕   Call waiting on conference calls is as bad as beeping pagers at the symphony.

✕   Conference calls are always better than an airplane seat.

✕   If you know you will be doing conference calls from home and you have children, dogs, or are undergoing a kitchen remodel, a phone with a mute button is the most important technical device ever. Saturday conference calls will guarantee barking dogs and crying children in the background.

✗ Joining a conference call from a cell phone will ruin the call for everyone, but sometimes you have to do it anyway.

✗ Unless it's a life-or-death matter, don't host a conference call from an airplane. If you're on a conference call from an airplane, everyone else on the call will lose your comments because they will:
  ⊘ Not be able to hear you.
  ⊘ Wonder who is paying for your call.
  ⊘ Pity the poor person sitting next to you.

✗ Conference calls will never be a legitimate excuse for not doing the things you are supposed to do. There is not a box for "did good conference calls" on your annual review.

✗ Never assume everyone has hung up from a conference call before you start a private conversation with those who admit to still being on the line.

✗ If there are more than five people on a conference call, figure out a way to determine whom the participants are other than asking who's on the call.

✗ Catch a conference call on audiotape sometime. Ask yourself if you would get up at 5:00 a.m. to listen to that voice. It could be time for elocution and enthusiasm lessons.

- A conference call is a premium time for multitasking; it may be your only chance to get work done.

- Conference calls with more than four people will mean one person does all the talking.

- Hit the mute button on the cell phone whenever you are on a conference call. Even if there is no background noise, there is for the others on the call. Know how to turn the mute button on and off quickly.

12

Don't Pat Short People on the Head

Ever sat next to someone in the bathroom and listened to him chat away on his cell phone, all the while wishing that the person on the other end knew what was happening? (This same scene may be replayed in the women's bathroom too, although I have no firsthand knowledge of such happenings.) Ever sat next to someone on an airplane, waiting to take off, while he or she was whispering into the phone about the intimacies of hooking up last night? Ever sat in a restaurant with a date while the person at the next table over carried on a conversation about a "deal" on his cell phone as if no one was sitting near him? Ever stood in line behind someone ordering six different kinds of coffees with chai and soy and extra hot and decaf foam, knowing that the order will be wrong and wondering how you know that but no one else does?

I am not an eavesdropper and I am not a coffee expert, but I sometimes wonder, "Is it me, or have people forgotten how to act?" Or, do they think others don't notice? Technologies and the push-pull of home and career demands have made life complex and stressful, but this is not an excuse to grow into a rude, insensitive jerk. If your courtesy and common sense quotient has atrophied, so probably has your career success and satisfaction. Whether the example is rude cell-phone usage, two-hundred-page PowerPoint presentations that no one will ever read, or heavy nasal breathing on conference calls, good judgment and proper behavior seem to be going in the wrong direction. This chapter is not a rant about cell-phone usage. It is, rather, a suggestion to take a deep breath and retool some simple ways that can make your career and your life better. I notice how others behave, and I am trying to point out that others notice how you deal with situations and how you treat others and that it is always important to do the right thing.

No lectures here about proper business etiquette. There are plenty of those bromides, although they only scratch the surface and talk about "them." I am talking about you. You who don't know what counts or don't pay attention to performance reviews. It's not too late to get some advice that no one else bothered to give you, and without guilt for those past sins. One of my many goals in life is to eliminate guilt, and I want you to be guilt free too. I want you to be aware and to change if you need to. I do want to show you some of the right ways and to be accountable for your own behavior. Your personal behavior, and probably your career, will never go from "good" to "great" if you are standing at the urinal talking on the phone.

Someday I want to stop asking myself, "Is it me or have people forgotten how to act?" I hope to do that by blurting out a few simple lessons in a fun and direct way.

- If you're with a client at Starbucks, don't order a decaf non-fat latte and then add sugar.

- Saying someone is "diverse" is about the same as saying he or she is gay, black, Latino, or something other than white. Avoid using the term that way.

- Give yourself enough time in the morning so you don't show up with pillow scars on your face.

- If your meal partner takes out a cell phone and puts it on the table, take yours out too. It's like putting the six-shooter on the table.

- When you hire a consultant, get the consultant jokes out of the way early or don't bring them up at all. The consultant has probably heard them all already.

- Don't pick your teeth with the business card of the client who just gave it to you.

- If someone asks you for the time, answer the question. Don't tell him or her how to build a watch.

- When you see someone from work away from work, such as at the supermarket, don't act like you just saw your teacher while playing hooky. Say hello and be relaxed.

- Table seating at business luncheons and dinners should be arranged in advanced.

- Don't pick your nose in your car, even if you're alone. Others do see you.

- When leaving a message for someone on his or her voice mail, always leave your number, even if he or she knows it.

- Talk about health problems only with your doctor.

- When someone sends you an announcement about a new job or a promotion, and you know the person, send him or her a note of congratulations. Even if you're dying inside.

- If you're married, wear your wedding ring.

- If you're a guest and you break something, don't even ask if you should replace it—just replace it.

- One thing you learn in college is: If it's free, eat it or drink it. Don't use that rule at work or at conferences. You're not at college anymore.

- Verify the pronunciation of people's names.

- At no time, under any circumstances, use a toothpick in public.

- If you take the last cup of coffee, at least take the pot off the burner. Make someone's life easier.

- Always be prepared with an appropriate toast and pre-meal blessing—and remember the words to the national anthem.

- Don't answer the phone by barking out your last name.

- After a hard project or long trip that has had you distracted, send flowers to your spouse or partner.

- Congratulate people who accomplish something, even if you haven't seen or talked to them in years.

- If people don't understand what you're saying, don't repeat it louder and slower.

- Dress conservatively; think maverick.

- Don't take your shoes off at work. Buy good shoes that fit instead.

- Steal Hilton Hotels' motto "We can do that." Don't steal from Hilton Hotels.

- One of the most irritating things children do is smack the newspaper when you're reading it. They're right; we're wrong.

- When talking to someone who speaks a foreign language, don't adopt his or her accent.

- Never ask anyone why he or she isn't married.

- In a meeting, talking on a cell phone is worse than carrying on a separate conversation.

- If you're always saying, "In other words," you're using the wrong words.

- Eat food with strong or bad odors anywhere but your office.

- Sin on the side of shaking hands too often, and introduce yourself to people who should know you.

- Take medication inconspicuously. Don't line up your pills on the lunchroom table. People will assume you have health issues.

- "That's a good question" is rarely necessary to say. "That's a bad question" is never necessary.

- Don't leave the newspaper on the bathroom floor. Don't take it in there in the first place.

- Flush is what we do in the bathroom, not the way we add more details, as in, "We are going to flesh out the proposal."

- If cab drivers want to talk, they'll let you know.

- With people you know but haven't seen for a while, take the risk and say hello. They'll remember too.

- Act as if you are someday going to run for public office.

- If it's too late to run for office, act that way anyway.

- People who work in high technology are always late. That's no excuse.

- Don't say, "Pardon my French." Either curse and mean it or don't curse at all.

- Don't be late for meetings. If you are late, don't make it a big deal with a complicated excuse; just apologize.

- Don't tell off-color jokes.

- If you tell a racist joke, be prepared to be fired.

✗   Return calls within twenty-four hours. Never leave one unanswered.

✗   If traveling on the corporate jet, know what the seating protocols are before you get on.

✗   Don't ever ask colleagues if they dye their hair. Don't ever tell them that they are fat or bald—or that they look tired.

✗   Don't eat garlic at lunch.

✗   Learn how to make proper introductions and then introduce people properly.

✗   Don't open any envelope or read any memo marked CONFIDENTIAL unless it's addressed to you.

✗   Never correct a coworker in front of a customer or client … or anyone else.

✗   Don't listen to rock and roll in your office.

✗   Graciousness always helps; when you have a visitor, make sure you offer soft drinks or coffee.

✗   Send thank-you notes to people who help you.

✶ When a relative or a friend has a baby, save the *New York Times* for the date and present it in the future as a gift.

✶ Never communicate anything important, such as "You're fired" or "I quit," over the cell phone or on voice mail.

✶ Treat everyone in the organization with respect and dignity whether it be the janitor or the president. Don't ever be patronizing.

✶ Don't use the speakerphone unless you're on a conference call.

✶ Don't treat people like they are dead if they get fired or laid off.

✶ Cigarette butts are litter. People who would never throw anything else on the ground believe a butt is not litter. It's not true.

✶ Annoying habits like blowing dust out of your glasses all the time can become your trademark. The same can be said for cracking your knuckles, smelling your fingers, twirling your hair, smacking your lips, picking your teeth or nose, belching and catching it in your mouth, and biting your nails. (What is that stuff anyway?)

- Don't wear T-shirts that say something that would offend your mother. Somebody's mother will see it.

- Worry about intimacy at work. If things seem to be getting a little chummy, they probably are, and people will notice. Don't give them something to talk about.

- Never play an iPod so loudly that the people around you can hear it.

- "Checking out" someone almost always gets noticed—if not by the checkee then by others in the area.

- Never eat anything bigger than your head.

- Never leave the men's room with your tie slung over your shoulder or tucked into your belt.

- It's one thing to learn from others and bend their ideas to your needs. It's quite another thing to steal their ideas and not give credit.

- Tell someone that you like him or her better than someone else at great peril—that information will be broadcast.

- Give people space when talking to them. Gomer Pyle never liked to listen to Sergeant Carter.

- The administrative staff is not a maid service. Clean up after yourself and don't leave dirty coffee cups in the sink or in the conference room.

- Don't chew on a pen before you give it to someone to use.

- Make sure your eyeglasses are right. It's hard to listen to someone when there are tear droppings all over the lenses. It's even worse if the glasses are crooked.

- If you fall asleep in a meeting, assume people will notice, no matter how many people are in attendance.

- After you feed your small children breakfast, check your cuffs, your elbows, and the seat of your pants for cereal before going to work. Cheerios tend to multiply and follow you.

- In talks with children it's best to change levels or lower your elevation, even if it means getting on your knees. In talking with people at work, do the same thing.

- Don't be afraid to show some emotion and conviction. Shake hands with people like you mean it.

- Make sure you don't leave the bathroom with little paper-towel balls all over your face.

- Never ask someone who stays home with children if he or she works.

✗   Belching and other bodily noises embarrass everyone around you. Don't do them.

✗   People who don't smoke also have strong feelings about secondhand smoke.

✗   Never clip your nails or pick your teeth where you can be seen or heard.

✗   Wearing earphones for a device doesn't give you the license to yell at those who are not.

✗   Have a short answer ready for the question "Where are you from?"

✗   Don't answer your phone if you are unable to speak to the caller—like when you have a roomful of people or a mouthful of food.

✗   Making grocery lists during staff meetings is in bad form. It will also make you hungry.

✗   If you're meeting someone for the first time in a social spot, know how to describe yourself in a non-self-aggrandizing way. "I'll be easy to spot; I look like Gwyneth Paltrow" is not a good descriptor.

✗   Never ask someone if you can pick his or her brains. You're not dealing with chicken bones.

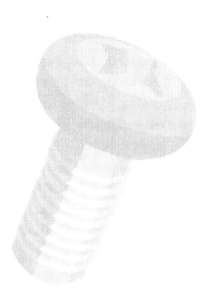

13

Making Forts with Blankets

When soon-to-be college graduates speak of the "real world," they envision a world full of bills; limited parking places that you have to pay for; no automatic IT support; getting up early every day or getting fired; getting semi-dressed up every day; no easily built-in set of friends; and no ATM in the form of parents. College graduates are correct in that assessment. The real world is the real world, and we all have to deal with it.

The real world has a lot of pluses, a lot of good things going for it, but those are usually placed in other categories like vacation or romance or family. The real world is more reserved for those activities that make you want to retreat back to college, no matter your age. The real world after college is more about people flipping you off from their cars for no apparent reason and cable guys who don't show up for hours, arrive when you go around the corner for a latte, and then charge you for a missed service call.

There is no antidote for the real world; we all just find our best ways of coping with it. For most of us, coping with it means dealing with it. As in, the real world is worse if you let your bills pile up rather than pay most of them occasionally. As in, when the guy in front of you in the coffee line orders an espresso drink that you know takes a long time and that the Barista will get it wrong and the guy will demand his money back, you order a drip coffee, not a latte. As in, do the things you may not like to do but have to do anyway so that you don't live in a world of dread, fear, and guilt. Dealing with the real world, rather than ignoring it, makes it a better real world. Surprisingly, it takes most of us a long time to figure this one out.

Death and taxes are not the only inevitable parts of life. The real world is too.

✗   Assume that anything you say out loud on your cell phone will get back to your children.

✗   Cell phones are the ultimate multitasking device. A phone (with headset) allows you to drive, drink a latte, and close a sales deal at the same time.

✗   Men who won't stop to ask for directions should not feel their manhood is jeopardized by using the cell phone to call for directions.

✖ "How are you?" is usually a greeting, not a real question. If it is really "How *are* you?" be alert; everyone thinks something is wrong.

✖ Workmen and contractors who show up when they say they will deserve a premium.

✖ E-mail allows you to keep old gangs together by sending out multiple messages to multiple people quickly—like reunions without the heavy drinking.

✖ Web-based reunion services will guarantee you receive mail from someone you don't want to hear from.

✖ Don't rub your eyes after reading the *New York Times*.

✖ "I erased it" are three of the sorriest words in any language. Other sorry words include, "I'm not a racist, but…" and "It hurts me to say this, but…"

✖ Rules from the work world that apply to all teenagers:
  ⊘ Always let someone know where you are.
  ⊘ Leaving a message on the answering machine doesn't mean you have permission.
  ⊘ Be home when you say you will. Period.
  ⊘ Know what is absolutely non-negotiable, like "Give me the keys."
  ⊘ If you're in trouble, don't negotiate.

- When you start recognizing the homeless people, feel bad for them; when they start recognizing you, give them money.

- Memorize the phone key pad so that you can spell names and dial numbers without looking at it.

- The most important question on a field trip or a benchmark trip is "Where is the souvenir shop?"

- When in a hurry, don't follow motorcycles through tollbooths; it takes riders a long time to get their money out of their pockets.

- Opening phrases of letters that invariably mean something disappointing is about to happen to you:
    - Due to the increased…
    - Due to the decreased…
    - Repeated attempts…
    - Based on our records…

- Don't interrupt people when they are talking to themselves.

- Never underestimate the power of a parking place or take it for granted.

- Never underestimate the wrath you can incur by taking more than one parking place.

✗ Ruts are easy to get into and difficult to get out of. Don't get stuck unless you want to.

✗ It's better to look for another pay phone than to wait for one to become available. If the pay phone next to you rings, don't answer it. It won't be for you.

✗ Sometimes procrastination can get you out of doing what you don't want to.

✗ Vacations always cost more than you think but less than they are worth.

✗ Remember the lesson of Beanie Babies. Otherwise rational people will do irrational and crazy things in the name of collecting strange items in the hopes of fast appreciation.

✗ Hold on to your Beanie Babies. They might be valuable for your grandchildren.

✗ Never transport a mattress or box spring on the roof of your car. There is plenty of evidence to support that one.

✗ Pack your children's lunches so that they will be the envy of the school.

✗ If you're in a spot where someone's cell phone rings annoyingly, make a dramatic point to turn yours off.

- Be sure to edit baby pictures that were taken in the hospital. The focus should be on babies, not birthing.

- Sometimes it pays to go to the doctor just to have a doctor.

- Have family meetings, especially before vacations or during crises.

- Altoids and TicTacs are in the same food group but neither counts as a meal.

- Metaphor dyslexia can be confusing but can get the point across:
  - Let's kill the cat in the bag with one stone.
  - The bull in the china shop is raising the tide.
  - Singing from the same roadmap.
  - Touching base is on the critical path.
  - Slow-moving targets for completion.
  - Calling to toss the bases with you.
  - Like shooting low-hanging fruit in a barrel.
  - The sky is falling into the frying pan.
  - We jumped from the frying pan onto the gravy train.
  - There are plenty of fish at the end of the rainbow.
  - Connecting the dots wins the game.
  - Too many cooks in the soup.
  - A straw man we want to tee up.
  - In my heart of hearts there is no silver bullet.

- If the only interesting mail you receive is addressed to the previous occupant, don't open the mail that is not addressed to you, change your life.

- If you announce that you collect something, make sure you really like it because you will get one on every birthday and holiday for the rest of your life. Think glass elephants and Thomas Kincaid plates.

- Register at Home Depot for your wedding gifts. The gifts will be used sooner and more often.

- Radio commercials with honking horns, sirens, or ringing phones should be illegal.

- W2 envy will drive you crazy and is not worthy of the brain space. And, like penis envy, there's not too much you can do about it.

- Forget the eye tests. DMV should give tests to see if people can talk on the phone and drive at the same time.

- Buying a more expensive scale won't make you lose weight. Buying a more expensive computer could make you more productive.

- "At the end of the day..." school gets out, nothing more or less.

- Never call a spouse a cost center.

- It is true. Sometimes you'll be on a roll and everything will click; take maximum advantage. When the opposite is true, hold steady and wait it out.

- Fountain pens always leak. Always. They leak more on airplanes.

- If you think people don't know what you are really after, think again.

- Pay parking tickets right away. The longer you wait, the more irritating they become.

- The lights on the dashboard of 90 percent of taxis read "check engine" or "see dealer." It's part of their code to let us know they live on the edge. Don't try it at home.

- Vacations are exactly equal to the enjoyment divided by the hassle to go and get there.

- Return any borrowed vehicle with a full tank of gas.

- Books written before 2000 still have value. Except for technology books.

- Having a vision is not the same as hallucinating. It may sometimes seem like hallucinogens are involved when the stated vision and goals are so remotely possible. The stretch goal needs to be believable. Most visions, missions, and strategic goals become nothing more than a daily reminder of a nebulous defeat. Make the vision embraceable and doable, something worth showing up for.

- Go to your child's plays, recitals, games, and special events even if the child is the youngest of ten.

- Recreational basketball does not give guys, regardless of the age, the license to get into fistfights.

- Vague promises about potential weekend plans cannot make up for missing birthdays, anniversaries, big games, or ballet recitals.

- When you're selling a car, give it a price as a starting point. "Best offer" only prolongs the negotiation.

- Don't teach your children how to swim or drive. Enroll them in swimming lessons and driver's education. It will eliminate tears and tantrums.

- Sometimes it's easier to change banks and open a new account than it is to reconcile your checkbook, but try to avoid that situation.

- Career counseling with your spouse or significant other is risky. If you're too direct, the perception can be that you're manipulative. If you're too permissive, it can appear that you don't care.

- Keep a journal, but not one in which you begin each page with "Dear Diary." Use a simple notebook where you make entries when something significant, interesting, or surprising happens. Someday it will help you answer the question "Where did all those years go?"

- Reading business and trade publications keeps you apprised of buzzwords and trends. Reading fiction keeps you balanced.

- If you drop names, make sure the target knows who you are talking about.

- More schooling never hurts. It may not have the immediate pay-off you want, but it's not going to hurt.

- If your friends accuse you of having a "Century-At-A-Glance" calendar, you may be too anal about planning your time.

- A concierge service is not necessarily a luxury. It is a way of telling people that time is important. Sometimes, no matter what it costs, if someone else will go to the DMV for you, it's worth it.

- Read your mail soon after you receive it.

✖ The only difference between a good haircut and a bad haircut is two weeks. The questions is "Can you endure two weeks?"

✖ Answer personal mail that you receive. E-mail may not count as a response.

✖ Name your children as if they were going to be president of the United States.

✖ Never be embarrassed about where you grew up, where you went to school, how you look, your name, or anything else that it's too late to fix. Be proud of who you are.

✖ Write letters or send postcards (even if they're from hotels) home to your children. Have them start a collection.

✖ The more your goal is to make life simple, the more it will go in the opposite direction.

✖ The true sign of being overworked is not overtime. It's stress.

✖ After particularly hard days, go home and build forts out of blankets with your children.

✖   Perceptions of message delivery vehicles:

   ⊘ US Mail – Slow but positive. Not only do you probably know the carrier, he or she just might bring a love letter, a check, or an eBay package.

   ⊘ E-mail – Neutral, sometimes threatening, sometimes joyful. It may be cluttered with messages from Nigerian princes and penis enlargement messages, but it can also have a note from an old friend or a positive customer.

   ⊘ Voice mail – Negative, the messages pile up, and it's always "Where is it?" or "Where are you?"

   ⊘ Overnight delivery – Positive, fast, and cheap and can save your professional life.

   ⊘ Children – Double positive. Always honest and loving.

✖   Make sure your children know you are proud of them.

✖   Be proud of your children, no matter what.

✖   Store your college textbooks with your parents until they announce they're moving. Then throw them away.

✖   Stay in touch with your best friends from high school and college.

✖   Know what your children are doing on the Internet—soon.

- Make up songs and stories for children. They won't know the difference and you'll feel creative.

- Take ballroom dancing lessons. They will be worth it even if the only time you ever use them is at your daughter's wedding.

- If you're really worried about something, ask yourself, "What's the worst that can happen to me?"

- If you keep your car radio set on SCAN on the way home from work, you need to chill out.

- Have your child take you to class as the exhibit for Sharing Time.

- A bad credit rating sticks with you for a long time—for you and your company.

- Leaders don't start anything without a vision of the outcome. Imagine Churchill going to the flip chart and turning to his staff and asking, "What do you think we should do?"

- Be proud of your name, whatever it is. Let people know what it is and how to pronounce it.

- When your children are asked what you do, if the only response they can muster is "Go to meetings," tell them again what you do.

✵   Researchers are finding relationships between physical attractiveness and success. Hang with the good-lookers.

✵   Leaving to catch a car pool is a legitimate reason to depart at a reasonable time.

✵   Car-pool with people you can at least talk to.

✵   If you are lining up all your bills every month and deciding which ones to pay, change your spending habits or change jobs.

✵   Learn to take two-minute vacations. Slow down to watch a child or a cloud.

✵   Never feel guilty about taking a vacation.

✵   When you ask someone how he or she gets so much done, the answer usually includes "I don't watch TV."

✵   Change your dream from a Porsche to a plush minivan as soon as you have children. It's not whether, it's when.

✵   Occasionally pay the toll for the driver behind you.

- Don't send your blue jeans to the dry cleaners. They will come back with a crease as if they'd been ironed and hurt the perceptions others have of you.

- When people give you the finger on the highway, don't let it hurt your feelings.

- Four dreaded words in any situation are: See attendant for key.

- Own stock in the company for which you work, but make sure not all the stock you own is in one company.

- Relationships change. Your one-time allies can become your nemeses. Remember who is who.

- If you're feeling sorry for yourself, do something, like delivering meals to the homebound, that will snap you out of it.

- Never appear stressed in front of a client, a customer, or your boss. Take a deep breath and ask yourself, "In the course of human events, how important is this?"

- Life is choices; always choose to do what you will remember ten years from now.

- Commuting is not necessarily bad—you just need a good reason for it, such as loving your job or loving your house. The longer the commute, the better the reason needs to be.

- Globalization is really happening.

- If you order a drink, name the label you want. Don't just say, "I'll have a scotch."

- Never pay a relative to fix your car. Never fix your relative's car. The car will always work better if it's taken to the shop. The same holds true for doing taxes, writing resumes, developing business plans, public relations, and all other business functions.

- Learn to enjoy the present and don't be too future-oriented. Your life will probably not change dramatically once you move from a Grade 9 to a Grade 11.

- When someone tells you these are the best years of your life, believe it and act accordingly. They are.

- Remember what it was like when you were waiting to sit at the grown-up table at Thanksgiving. When you deal with the "new kids" in the organization, think of what it was like when you were finally invited to change seats.

- If one of your colleagues shows up wearing exactly the same thing you're wearing, do something that won't have you next to each other all day.

✗ Assume that little aluminum ketchup packets will always spill on your clothes. Any Mexican food will end up on your clothes.

✗ If the shampoo comes in a little aluminum packet, open it before you hop in the shower and get your hands wet.

✗ Every once in a while, surprise your spouse and meet him or her at the airport. It will be a much appreciated surprise.

✗ Worry about intimacy within your family and in relationships. If you believe you're losing it, you probably are.

✗ If you're not sure if the tie or the shoes match, they don't. If you're not sure if it's dressy enough for business casual, it's not. Wear something else.

✗ Remember that lots of other people are reading the same advice that you are about stock picks. Do your own homework as well.

✗ One of the highest compliments you can be paid is to be called a Renaissance person.

✗ Great ideas and solutions to problems often occur right before you fall asleep at night. Get up and write them down or they will be lost in the morning.

- Sloppiness always costs money or time.
- Learn from our friends in Washington: Nothing gets accomplished unless people listen to each other and are willing to make compromises for a common goal.
- Never take credit for an idea that is not your own.
- Nightmares where you go to jail or get hurt will help you appreciate the fact that you're free and healthy. If you feel sorry for yourself, eat an anchovy pizza right before you go to bed.
- Photos of dogs are not equivalent to photos of children.
- Smelling something burning is never a good sign.
- The only college textbooks you should not throw away are *Introduction to Art History*, *Introduction to Statistics*, and *Comparative Religions*.
- There is no greater joy than going home to hear the patter of little feet and voices screaming with glee rushing to meet you.
- Don't name your children anything that is likely to be confused with the names of dogs, horses, or vegetables.

- Save decorative stationery for personal notes. Kittens and balloons will not help you in the business world.

- In stressful situations, a little humor will tell people you haven't lost touch with reality.

- The "permanent record" is a powerful and mystical tool. Don't let it intimidate you.

- Never get drunk with someone who can fire you.

- Saving plastic bags will lead to huge plastic bags full of plastic bags that you eventually throw away. They breed.

- Taking the garbage out to the curb, knowing it will be picked up, might be the closest thing you get to closure week in and week out.

- The time value of money does not mean that the more time you spend worrying about money, the more money you have.

- Make sure to give short speeches after dinners where people have been drinking. Very short.

- Buy building blocks for your children and other toys that they can pass along to their children.

- Spend Sunday mornings in quiet time.

✖ At the end of a great week, when you get in the car, put in the long version of "Stairway to Heaven" and play it as loud as it will go.

✖ The Monday blahs are a reality. Scientists are saying it's because of what we eat and drink on weekends. Don't change what you eat or drink—just set realistic expectations for Monday.

✖ Work hard on Friday so that you never feel guilty on Sunday evening for what you didn't do last week.

✖ Saying "You better drive" is a sign of maturity.

✖ Always buy the property when playing Monopoly.

✖ Fall in love with a dog owner; he or she will be home at night.

✖ Time-outs work only with children.

✖ If you play golf, use good equipment—bought, begged, or borrowed. Don't get the old, faded red plaid bag off the hook in the garage.

✖ Maintain outside interests—volunteer weekends in not-for-profits and stay physically fit.

✖ Take all vacations and long weekends. Never let vacation time expire.

✗   Make time for life outside of work.

✗   You will never regret having spent too much time with your kids.

✗   Bring your kids to the office so they can see where you work.

✗   Just because you are in business and have a family doesn't mean you can't be in shape—it actually makes it even more important.

✗   Don't work on weekends—work longer during the week if you have to.

✗   Give the in-laws lottery tickets for their birthdays.

✗   If you don't have time to coach the Little League team, either make the time, get lots and lots of help, or don't volunteer.

✗   If you go out to dinner with a group and you don't have cash, don't think people won't notice when you put the entire bill on a credit card that rewards you with frequent flyer miles.

✗   Give surprise birthday parties only for those who will appreciate them. Let them know in advance.

- Acknowledge that your time is valuable and that to experience balance and get more accomplished, you may have to pay for help.

- When you go to family reunions, be prepared to easily describe what you do.

- Your diet isn't working until someone asks you if you've been losing weight.

- Take too many photos of your children. Print out the best digital photos.

- Watch the movie *Father of the Bride* if you have a daughter. It will help you prepare.

- Consider the hassle-to-enjoyment ratio before you do anything like go away for a weekend. Create numerators and denominators of life.

- If the water must be shut off to do a repair, you need a plumber. If the electricity must be shut off, you need an electrician.

- When jogging, assume all untethered dogs will bite you. Assume all dogs that look or sound mean are not tied up.

- People will see you in your car when you're singing, playing the air guitar, or drumming on the steering wheel. Do it anyway.

- You know you've made it when you have a vacation home and time to enjoy it.

- If you absolutely must work on a weekend, do it on Saturday. If you absolutely have to study on a weekend, do it on Sunday.

- Give money to street performers that you enjoy.

- Listen to Copeland's "Fanfare for the Common Man" every Monday morning.

EPILOGUE:
THE LAWS OF CONVERGENCE

The Laws of Convergence first occurred to me while sitting on an airplane next to a guy with the same name as me reading the same book and the havoc it caused to the airline. Convergence is real, and here is how it plays out.

Every morning when I go to the front porch in my bathrobe to get the newspaper, someone is out front walking his or her dog. It's not necessarily the same person, but it is an "automatic" that someone will be there.

At the office, when I have to go to the bathroom, my boss is already in there.

The word *convergence* conjures up a somewhat mystical concept. To some, it is a special intersection, a miraculous point in time when the technology industry, the communications industry, and the media industry all get together to share content and technology so that we can watch *The Simpsons* reruns anytime we want on any device we want, including the backs of our eyelids. To others it means that through an unending course of miracles one system will converge with another and stop an unending sequence of duplicative and redundant systems, as in, "Someday our systems will converge so that we will know whether or not we are making money and how many employees we have."

To me, convergence is the best way to describe things that you know will happen, no matter what. Convergence is not good or bad, it just is. No matter how many times a presentation is reviewed, it will be revised at the last minute, which will make life hell for everyone who worked on it. No matter how long in advance the presentation is done and approved, someone will be at Kinko's at 3:00 a.m. getting colored copies made and bound. Murphy's Laws are all about what went wrong. Convergence Laws are just about the givens.

There are millions of Convergence Laws that we live with every day. The telemarketer will always call just as you sit down to dinner. One of the kids will always be off from school for a teachers' workshop when everyone else has major events that day and can't stay home. The flight will always be late when you have a connection to make, which will induce severe anxiety for the first leg of the flight and a sprint through the airport when you are most dressed up to meet your loved one.

Bear with convergence and know it when you see it. Convergence is the way to see connections between meetings and your job. Convergence is the way to understand how your cell phone allows you to attend your daughter's soccer game. Convergence is when you get a promotion when you least expect it. Convergence fulfills your destiny so that when you are ready to take a job offer, you are notified that you are being laid off. Convergence is what it is.

Moran's Law of Convergence

- Two cars going in the opposite direction will always pass at the narrowest point in the road. If there's a bicyclist on the same road, the chances of all three passing at the same point are increased.

- The maid will always be at your hotel room when you go to it at break time. If you really have to use the bathroom, the odds are increased.

- If you want to see something from the road, a bus or eighteen-wheeler will pass and get in your way at the exact moment you could have seen it.

- The car will always be parked on top of the hose.

- Toll takers will always change shifts in your lane when it is your time to pay.

- Conversation with a child will always start immediately after they dive under water.

- Morning walkers will always be passing by when you go to get the newspaper in your underwear.

- Evening special events that you want to attend will always be scheduled at the same time. If you haven't been out in a long time, there is a multiplier effect at work here.

- While taking a photo, someone will walk between you and your subject at the exact time of the click of the shutter.

- Two families leaving a restaurant at the same time will invariably be parked next to each other.

- No matter the size of the parking lot, someone will be leaving or pulling into the spot next to yours at the same time.

- The letter will always run over so that only one line is on page two.

- The toilet paper will always run out when it's your turn.

- The pilot will always tell you where you are and talk over the movie soundtrack at the most critical point of the movie.

- When pressing the button for the classical music station, it will always be during the three seconds of silence between movements and you turn it up much louder to see what's wrong.

- While on a cell phone in your car, the most critical part of the conversation will occur while going through a tunnel or as you enter the underground parking garage. Or the Harley will always be riding next to you at the most critical point of the conversation.

- The more you have to go to the bathroom, the greater the likelihood that the cart will be blocking the aisle.

- The windshield wipers always work until it rains.

- When traveling by air with children, you will always be assigned to sit in the emergency row, the one place you can't sit without causing great commotion when you board.

- The cursor will always block the spot on the computer screen that you need to see.

- The cashier always needs to change the tape in the register when it's your turn to pay. The fewer the items, the greater the likelihood.

- Call-waiting will happen every time you're on the phone.

- The cash in your wallet will always run out when you need a taxi the most.

- The car in front of you will always take the one parking place that's open.

- Your cell phone will always ring while you're in the bathroom.

- The gas tank will be on E when you can least afford to stop without being even later.

- You will always be the busiest at work when you least want to be.

- The clothes you need the most will always be at the cleaners. The cleaners will be closed.

- The alarm on your house will always go off when you are on vacation—at 2:00 a.m.

- The hot water will always run out when it's time to rinse the shampoo out of your hair.

- The delivery person will always arrive when you're gone for five minutes.

The Driveway Convergence Conundrum

- When you pull into a driveway to turn around, the owner will be standing in the garage.

- When you pull into your own driveway, a walked dog will invariably be going to the bathroom there.

- When you're backing out of your own driveway, someone will be walking behind your car.

- When you're backing out of your own driveway, the neighbor across the street will also be backing out of his or her driveway.

- When a workman moves his pickup truck to get out of your way, he will pull into your driveway.

Converse Convergence

The law of converse convergence is when you want something to be there, and it isn't:

- When up a little early, the newspaper won't be there.

- If you're early for a flight, it will be delayed. If you're late in arriving at the airport, the flight will take off on time.

- You will always be on the left side of the airplane when the tourist attractions are on the right.

Convergence at Work

Convergence can be a happy coincidence of variables coming together, or it can give you claustrophobia. It can help impossible projects reach early success, or it can delay projects for years due to little things happening at the same time. It can be a joyous occasion, or it can make you miserable. Be ready for convergence, make the best of it, and recognize it as a part of the world at work and all around you.

Printed in the United States
72930LV00001B/115-600